CONTENTS

WALKING TOURS

New York

Rena Bulkin

MACMILLAN • USA

ABOUT THE AUTHOR

Rena Bulkin began her travel-writing career when she set out for Europe in search of adventure. She found it writing about hotel and restaurants for the *New York Times* International Edition. She has since authored 15 travel guides to far-flung destinations.

MACMILLAN TRAVEL

A Simon & Schuster Macmillan Company
1633 Broadway
New York, NY 10019

ISBN 0-02-860470-9
ISSN 1081-339X

Editor: Lisa Renaud
Editorial Assistant: Robin Michaelson
Map Editor: Douglas Stallings
Design by Amy Peppler Adams—designLab, Seattle
Maps by Ortelius Design

SPECIAL SALES

Bulk purchases (10+ copies) of Frommer's travel guides are available to corporations at special discounts. The Special Sales Department can produce custom editions to be used as premiums and/or for sales promotion to suit individual needs. Existing editions can be produced with custom cover imprints such as corporate logos. For more information, write to: Special Sales, Simon & Schuster, 1230 Avenue of the Americas, New York, NY 10020.

Manufactured in the United States of America

LIST OF MAPS

The Walking Tours

An Invitation to the Readers

In researching this book, I have come across many wonderful sights and restaurants, the best of which I have included here. As you explore New York, please share your experience, especially if you want to bring to my attention information that has changed since this book was researched. You can address your letters to:

Rena Bulkin
Frommer's Walking Tours: New York
Macmillan Travel
1633 Broadway
New York, NY 10019

An Additional Note

Please be advised that travel information is subject to change at any time. The author, editors, and publisher cannot be held responsible for the experiences of readers while traveling. Your safety is important to us, however, so we encourage you to stay alert and be aware of your surroundings. Keep a close eye on cameras, purses, and wallets, all favorite targets of thieves and pickpockets.

INTRODUCING NEW YORK

In his novels, British humorist
P. G. Wodehouse often talked about people who made the mistake of confusing the unlikely with the impossible. Obviously, these errant individuals were not New Yorkers. In the Big Apple—as in Wodehouse's anarchic world—the unlikely happens daily and the impossible with considerable regularity. To step out for a stroll on this city's streets is to stray from the rigid pathways of mundane reality. No city has New York's energy and verve—and none can match its frenetic and zany street life.

MIXED NUTS & MICHELANGELOS

For openers, a sizable cast of regular characters inhabits the city's streets. Strolling about, you might encounter the Tree Man, who is always festooned with leafy branches; the portly fellow with a long white beard who dresses as Santa Claus the year round (he's Jewish, no less); or the man who pushes a baby carriage whose occupant is a large white duck!

One of New York's most memorable street people was Moondog, a hulking blind man who spent the 1960s standing sentinel at the corner of 53rd Street and Sixth Avenue—dressed as a Viking. Occasionally, journalists did stories about him and it was revealed that as he stood there statuelike, leaning on a wooden staff, he was composing music in his head. On a lark, a Columbia record company executive (their offices were close by) decided to bring him into the studio to cut an album. It sold pretty well, and, with the profits, Moondog bought a house upstate and retired from New York's roster of outdoor eccentrics. There are many ways to make it in this town.

Quentin Crisp once said, "Everyone in Manhattan is a star or a star manqué, and every flat surface in the island is a stage." Street performers abound here. They run the gamut from a tuxedoed gent who does Fred-and-Ginger ballroom dances with a life-size rag doll (usually in front of the Metropolitan Museum) to the circus-caliber acrobats and stand-up comics who garner large audiences in Washington Square Park. There are mimes and musicians—everything from steel drum bands to classical string quartets to Ecuadoran flute players. If there's a line at a movie theater, waiting patrons may be entertained by jugglers and fire eaters—or perhaps a pianist with his candelabra-adorned baby grand perched atop a truck.

We even have freelance street artists. You may note here and there (especially in the East Village) lovely little mosaic-tile designs adorning the sidewalk and streetlight pedestals. An area artist created them from cracked plates and crockery picked up from people's trash. In the early 1980s—to everyone's delight— someone printed purple footsteps and stenciled beautiful animal and fish designs on sidewalks throughout Manhattan. On a more sinister note, a few years back, someone painted body outlines everywhere similar to the chalk markings police use to delineate corpses of murder victims. There was one on my street, atop which a local wag had written, "I've fallen and I can't get up."

One could go on *ad infinitum* with these New York stories. Our streets are a free outdoor theater with ongoing performances 24 hours a day. Whatever else you may feel walking around this town, you will never be bored. But even without eccentric behavior and gratis entertainment, the ever pulsating streets of New York would yield up endless excitement.

TWIN TOWERS, TENEMENTS & TOWN HOUSES

In doing these walks, you'll come to appreciate that New York is a city of extraordinary architecture. The Financial District's neo-classic "temples"—embellished with allegorical statuary, massive

The Tours at a Glance

Riverside Park

96th St.

86th St.

FDR Drive

79th St.

The Upper East Side

72nd St.

Columbus Ave.

Broadway

The Upper West Side

5th Ave.

1st Ave.

Roosevelt Island

Queens

Central Park

59th St.

West End Ave.

8th Ave.

Midtown

Lexington Ave.

Queensboro Bridge

42nd St.

Times Square

34th St.

11th Ave.

Empire State Building

23rd St.

Broadway

East River

14th St.

Greenwich Village Literary Tour II

Greenwich Village Literary Tour I

The EastVillage

Hudson River

Houston St.

The Lower East Side

Williamsburg Bridge

West Side Hwy.

Canal St.

Chinatown

Manhattan Bridge

Chambers St.

(278)

Broadway

BQE

Flatbush Ave.

Lower Manhattan/ The Financial District

Brooklyn Bridge

Brooklyn Heights

Court St.

Battery Park

South Street Seaport

Ferries to Ellis Island/ Statue of Liberty

Atlantic Ave.

Brooklyn

9662

colonnades, vaulted domes, and vast marble lobbies—stand side by side with the soaring skyscrapers that make up the world's most famous skyline. Close by—in the revitalized South Street Seaport district—sailing ships and seafood markets form a scenic backdrop to quaint cobblestoned streets lined with early 19th-century warehouses, hotels, and saloons in Georgian and Federal architectural styles. Across the bridge are the tranquil tree-shaded streets of Brooklyn Heights—a charming enclave of brownstones, churches, and landmark buildings, with a riverside promenade offering scenic views of the Manhattan skyline and the Statue of Liberty. The history of immigrant groups is manifest in the ramshackle tenements of Chinatown and the Lower East Side. In Greenwich Village, you'll see the stately Greek Revival town houses where Henry James and Edith Wharton lived. And uptown, magnificent private mansions built for the Vanderbilts and the Whitneys overlook Central Park, itself one of the world's most impressive urban greenbelts. No wonder quintessential New Yorker Woody Allen was inspired to pay loving tribute to the city's architectural diversity by including an otherwise gratuitous tour of his favorite buildings in the movie *Hannah and Her Sisters.*

THE NEIGHBORHOODS: BOK CHOY, BEADS & BOHEMIANS

Though it's been called more of a boiling than a melting pot, New Yorkers cherish the ethnic diversity of city neighborhoods. Going from one part of town to another is an adventure almost akin to foreign travel. From the days of the early Dutch settlers, immigrants have striven to recreate their native environments in selected neighborhoods. Hence, the restaurants of Mulberry Street, with convivial cafés spilling onto the sidewalks, very much evoke the streets of Rome—especially during frequent Italian festivals when those sidewalks are crowded with vendors selling hot sausages, calzone, and cannoli.

There are two Little Indias—one along Lexington Avenue from about 27th to 30th Streets, the other, which New Yorkers call "Indian restaurant street," on East 6th Street between First and Second Avenues. The latter's cozy curry houses (there are at least a dozen) combine cheap but very hearty meals with exotic ambience—even live sitar music at dinner. The East Village also has a sizable Ukrainian population, whose inexpensive restaurants (featuring borscht, blini, and pierogi) enhance the local culinary scene. Ukranian folk arts—such as intricately painted Easter eggs, beautifully embroidered peasant blouses, and illuminated manuscripts—are displayed in local shops and even warrant a museum on Second Avenue.

Orthodox Jews still operate shops that evolved from turn-of-the-century pushcarts along cobblestoned Orchard Street. This colorful quarter not only offers superb discount shopping—and a chance to exercise your *hondling* (bargaining) skills—it provides an opportunity to sample the flavor of New York in the form of a pastrami on rye at Katz's Delicatessen.

Chinatown—home to more than 160,000 Chinese—is probably New York's most extensive ethnic area, and it's continually expanding, gobbling up parts of the old Lower East Side and Little Italy. Its narrow, winding streets are lined with noodle shops, Chinese vegetable vendors, small curio stores, Buddhist temples, Chinese movie theaters, and several hundred restaurants. New Yorkers don't talk about going out for Chinese food—they opt for Szechuan, Hunan, Cantonese, Mandarin, Fukien, or dim sum.

I could go on and on. There are Hispanic, Czech, German, Greek, Hungarian, Russian, Arab, and West Indian parts of town as well.

But ethnic groups are not the only factor defining New York neighborhoods. Around Broadway from Macy's to about 39th Street you're in the heart of the Garment District, where most of America's fabric and clothing designers maintain offices. In this bustling area, artists race through the streets carrying large portfolios of next season's designs, trying not to collide with workers pushing racks of already extant clothing. Also distinct are the city's bead, book, feather, fur, flower, toy, diamond, and, of course, theater districts.

Different neighborhoods also attract diverse residents. The Upper East Side is where old money lives, while rumpled intellectuals are more likely to call the Upper West Side home. Young trendies and aging hippies live in the East Village, old Bohemians in the West Village. The West Village and Chelsea are home to sizable gay populations. These are not hard and fast rules, but each area does have a distinct flavor. You probably won't find designer clothing on St. Marks Place. On the other hand, a Madison Avenue boutique is unlikely to carry S&M

leatherwear. Midtown is the city's main shopping area, site of our ever-diminishing grand department stores. And Broadway dissects the town diagonally; though it's most famous for the glitz and glitter of the Great White Way, it actually spans Manhattan from Battery Park to the Bronx.

IF YOU CAN MAKE IT HERE . . .

The song has become a cliché, but like many clichés it's true. New York is, and always has been, a mecca for the ambitious. It is a city where achievement is practically a prerequisite for social acceptability. And though only a small percentage of the ardently aspiring become famous—or even manage to eke out a living in their chosen fields—the effort keeps New Yorkers keen-witted, intense, on the cutting edge.

It's not easy to be a big fish in this pond, but it's the only pond really worth swimming in. New York is America's business and financial center, where major deals have gone down over power lunches since the days when Thomas Jefferson and Alexander Hamilton chose the site for the nation's capital over a meal at a Manhattan restaurant. Every major book and magazine publisher is based here. It's an international media and fashion center. New York galleries set worldwide art trends. And a lead in a play in Galveston, Texas, is less impressive than a bit part on Broadway. (At least New Yorkers think so.)

For that reason, almost every famous artist, writer, musician, and actor has, at one time or another, resided in Gotham. The waitress serving you in a coffee shop may be tomorrow's Julia Roberts; your cab driver may make the cover of *Time*. And since they're all over town, you'll probably even rub elbows with an already-acclaimed celebrity or two as well. If not, there's always the thrill of downing a drink or two in bars that Dylan Thomas or Jackson Pollock frequented, visiting the Greenwich Village haunts of the Beat Generation, peering up at what was once Edgar Allan Poe's bedroom window, or dining at the Algonquin Hotel where Round Table wits Dorothy Parker, Alexander Woollcott, and George S. Kaufman traded barbs in the 1920s.

All of the above makes it very difficult for New Yorkers to find lasting happiness anywhere else. The presence of so many movers and shakers gives New York tremendous vitality and sophistication. When you study film at the New School your lecturers are Martin Scorsese, Norman Jewison, Sydney Pollack, Barry Levinson, and Neil Simon. Pavarotti's at one Met, everyone from Raphael to Rembrandt at the other. No other bookstore in America is as wonderful as the Strand, no food store as alluring as Zabar's (except perhaps Balducci's or Dean & Deluca), no department store a match for Bloomie's, no mall comparable to Orchard Street. Where else can you easily satisfy a craving for Thai noodles at 10 o'clock in the evening? Or have your choice of dozens of movies nightly, many of which will never play in most American towns?

Visitors from the hinterlands may question how we stand the constant noise, the rudeness, the filth, the outrageous rents, the crime, the crazies, or even one another. But though New Yorkers frequently talk about leaving the city, few ever do. We've created a unique frame of reference, and it doesn't travel well. We take the bizarreness of life here and translate it into black humor. The constant stimulation feeds our creativity, and other people and places seem bland by comparison. To quote theatrical impresario Joseph Papp, "Creative people get inspiration from their immediate environment, and New York has the most immediate environment in the world."

I'm a lifelong New Yorker—one who often gripes about the city and talks of moving to more peaceful precincts. But in writing these walking tours, I've fallen in love with New York all over again. It's like a love affair with Mr. Wrong—he's moody, unpredictable, not someone you can bring home to Mom, and bad for you in the bargain—but infinitely more attractive and exciting than anyone else. Who could leave?

Lower Manhattan/ The Financial District

Start: The Municipal Building, at Centre and Chambers Streets.

Subway: Take the 4, 5, or 6 to Brooklyn Bridge/City Hall, or take the N or R to City Hall. (You can also catch an M-15 City Hall bus on Second Avenue.)

Finish: The New York Stock Exchange.

Time: Approximately 3 to 4 hours.

Best Time: Any weekday, when the wheels of finance are spinning and lower Manhattan is a maelstrom of frantic activity.

Worst Time: Weekends, when most buildings are closed.

The narrow winding streets of the Financial District occupy the earliest-settled area of Manhattan, where the Dutch established the colony of Nieuw Amsterdam

8

in the early 17th century. Before their arrival, downtown was part of a vast forest—a lush hunting ground for its Native American residents, inhabited by mountain lions, bobcats, beavers, white-tailed deer, and wild turkeys. A tribal warpath—that later evolved into Broadway—extended from the Battery to the present City Hall Park.

Today this section of the city, much like Nieuw Amsterdam, centers on commerce. Wall Street is America's most cogent symbol of money and power; bulls and bears have replaced the wild beasts of the forest, and conservatively attired lawyers, stockbrokers, bankers, and businesspeople have supplanted the Native Americans and earnest Dutchmen who once traded otter skins and beaver pelts on these very streets.

A highlight of this tour is the Financial District's diverse architecture, in which the neighborhood's most modern manifestations and its grand historical structures are dramatically juxtaposed: Colonial, 18th-century Georgian/Federal, and 19th-century neoclassical buildings stand in the shadow of the colossal skyscrapers that form the silhouette of the world's most famous skyline. The starkly soaring twin icons that comprise the World Trade Center rise near the Gothic opulence of the Woolworth Building, a self-conceived monument to a mogul of finance; New York's quaint post-Colonial City Hall contrasts with the boldly neoclassic Beaux Arts grandeur of the Municipal Building nearby.

To best view the buildings described below, stand far back to gain aesthetic perspective, then move closer to inspect the architectural detail of facades and interior spaces.

• • • • • • • • • • • • • • • • •

Starting Out   Consider starting out early with breakfast at **Ellen's Café & Bake Shop,** 270 Broadway, at Chambers Street (tel. 962-1257). Owner Ellen Hart won the Miss Subways beauty pageant in 1959, and her restaurant walls are lined with her own and other Miss Subways posters, plus photographs of all the politicians who eat here—Al D'Amato, Rudy Giuliani, Bella Abzug, Andy Stein, Mario Cuomo, and Geraldine Ferraro, to name just a few. Muffins, biscuits, and pastries are all oven fresh, and, of course, full breakfasts of eggs, bacon, pancakes, and even eggs Benedict and Belgian waffles are available. Ellen's opens at 6:30am weekdays, 8am Saturdays; it's closed on Sundays.

1. **The Municipal Building,** a grand civic edifice built between 1909 and 1914 to augment City Hall's government office space, was designed by the famed architectural firm of McKim, Mead, and White (as in Stanford White). They utilized Greek and Roman design elements such as a massive Corinthian colonnade, ornately embellished vaults and cornices, and allegorical statuary. A triumphal arch, its barrel-vaulted ceiling adorned with bas-relief panels, forms a magnificent arcade over Chambers Street; it has been called the "gate of the city." Sculptor Adolph Weinman created many of the building's bas-reliefs, medallions, and allegorical groupings of human figures (they symbolize civic pride, progress, guidance, prudence, and executive power). The heroic, and very charming, hammered-copper statue of Civic Fame that tops the structure 582 feet above the street was also designed by Weinman. Holding a crown, its five turrets symbolic of the five boroughs of New York, she balances gracefully atop a globe. This is, by the way, Manhattan's largest statue.

   See many lovey-dovey couples walking in and out? The city's marriage license bureau is on the second floor, and a wedding takes place about every 20 minutes in the chapel across the hall.

   Cross Centre Street and walk west on Chambers Street to:

2. **Surrogate's Court (The Hall of Records),** 31 Chambers Street. Housed in this sumptuous turn-of-the-century Beaux Arts structure—its grand design intended to evoke civic pride—are all the legal records relating to Manhattan real estate deeds and court cases, some dating back to the mid-1600s. (Surrogate judges deal with estates of deceased persons.) Heroic statues of distinguished New Yorkers (Peter Stuyvesant, De Witt Clinton, and others) front the mansard roof, and the doorways, surmounted by arched pediments, are flanked by Philip Martiny's sculptural groups portraying *New York in Revolutionary Times* (to your left) and *New York in Its Infancy* (to your right). Above the

Lower Manhattan/The Financial District

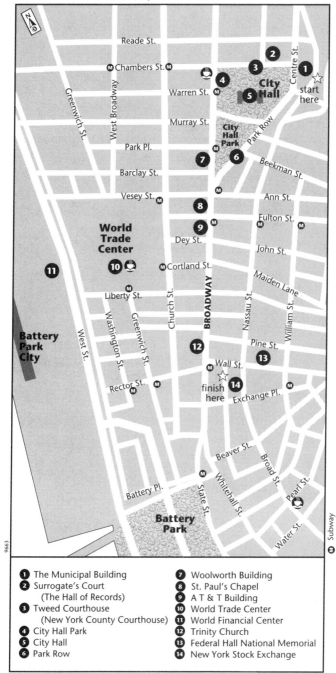

- ❶ The Municipal Building
- ❷ Surrogate's Court
     (The Hall of Records)
- ❸ Tweed Courthouse
     (New York County Courthouse)
- ❹ City Hall Park
- ❺ City Hall
- ❻ Park Row
- ❼ Woolworth Building
- ❽ St. Paul's Chapel
- ❾ A T & T Building
- ❿ World Trade Center
- ⓫ World Financial Center
- ⓬ Trinity Church
- ⓭ Federal Hall National Memorial
- ⓮ New York Stock Exchange

entrance is a three-story Corinthian colonnade. Walk around the building to view all of its allegorical sculptural adornments.

Then step inside to see the magnificent lobby's beautiful murals and arched mosaic ceiling; the latter is embellished with astrological symbols, Egyptian and Greek motifs, and figures representing retribution, justice, sorrow, and labor. Continue back to the three-story skylit central hall with its colonnaded rotunda and ornate staircase adapted from the foyer of the Grand Opera House in Paris.

Diagonally across the street at 52 Chambers is:

3. **Tweed Courthouse** (New York County Courthouse). This 1872 Italianate courthouse was built during the tenure of William Marcy "Boss" Tweed, who, in his post on the Board of Supervisors, stole millions in construction funds. Originally budgeted as a $250,000 job in 1861, the courthouse project escalated to the staggering sum (for the 19th century) of $14 million. Bills were padded to an unprecedented extent. For instance, Andrew Garvey, who was to become known as the "Prince of Plasterers," was ostensibly paid $45,966.89 for a single day's work! The ensuing scandal (Tweed and his cronies, it came out, had pocketed at least $10 million) wrecked Tweed's career, and he died penniless in jail.

Today a somewhat shabby city government office building, the courthouse is fronted by a Corinthian-columned portico. Its marble-floored lobby, under a restored rotunda, houses an art gallery, which is open Monday through Friday from 9am to 5pm. Walk in and take a look around.

Walking toward Broadway, make a left into triangular:

4. **City Hall Park,** a 250-year-old green surrounded by landmark buildings. Northeast of City Hall in the park is a statue of Horace Greeley (seated with newspaper in hand) by John Quincy Adams Ward. Another statue (southwest of City Hall), by Frederick MacMonnies, depicts Nathan Hale at age 21, having just uttered his famous words before execution: "I only regret that I have but one life to lose for my country." This small park has been a burial ground for paupers and the site of public executions, parades, and protests.

It is the setting for:

5. **City Hall,** the seat of municipal government, housing the offices of the mayor and his staff, the City Council, and other city agencies. One of the most delightful buildings in Manhattan, it combines Georgian and French Renaissance styles. Designed by Joseph F. Mangin and John McComb, Jr., it went up between 1803 and 1811. Later additions include the clock and 6,000-pound bell in the cupola tower. The cupola itself is crowned with a stately white-painted copper statue of *Justice*; classically draped, she holds a scale in one hand, a sword in the other. Believe it or not, she was factory produced; her creator is unknown.

It was on this site (then the City Common) that George Washington read the Declaration of Independence on July 9, 1776, officially bringing New York into the Revolutionary War. When Lincoln lay in state outside City Hall after his assassination in 1865, 120,000 New Yorkers came to pay him tribute. And it is on City Hall steps that New York mayors bestow the keys to the city on honored guests.

Barring days when there are demonstrations or special hearings that draw large crowds, you can enter the building between 10am and 4pm, Monday through Friday. Several areas are open to the public, beginning with the Corinthian-columned lobby, which centers on a resplendent coffered and skylit rotunda. The elegant Governor's Room upstairs—where Lafayette was received in 1824—houses a museum containing Washington's writing desk, his inaugural flag, and artwork by well-known American artists such as John Trumbull; this room is closed from noon to 1pm. City Hall contains quite an impressive collection of American art, by the way; in your wanderings, you might note works by George Caitlin, Thomas Sully, Samuel B. Morse, and Rembrandt Peale, among others. You can also view the Public Hearing Chambers and the Council Chambers.

The eastern boundary of City Hall Park is:

6. **Park Row.** In the early 20th century, 12 New York City newspapers—all the great metropolitan dailies—maintained offices on this street.

On the other side of the park is the:

7. **Woolworth Building.** This soaring "Cathedral of Commerce" cost Frank W. Woolworth $13.5 million worth of nickels and dimes in 1913. Designed by Cass Gilbert, it was, until 1930—when surpassed by the Chrysler Building—the world's tallest edifice. Its advent was hailed with pomp and ceremony: At its opening, President Woodrow Wilson pressed a button from the White House that illuminated the building's 80,000 electric lightbulbs! The architectural style is neo-Gothic, with spires, gargoyles, flying buttresses, vaulted ceilings, 16th-century–style lace-in-stone traceries, castlelike turrets, and a churchlike interior.

Examine the seemingly infinite detail on the entrance archway, including the classical figures of Mercury (symbol of commerce) on the top left and Ceres (goddess of grain) on the top right. Then step into the lofty marble entrance arcade to view the gleaming mosaic ceiling and gold-leafed cornices. The corbels (carved figures under the crossbeams) in the lobby include whimsical portraits of Woolworth counting coins and Gilbert holding a miniature model of the building. Note, too, the grand marble staircase and balustrade at the end of the entrance corridor and Paul Jennewein's murals of Commerce and Labor on the mezzanine.

On the 28th floor you can view Woolworth's collection of company memorabilia (e.g., Woolworth's mahogany desk) and Napoleonic objects. Woolworth, an admirer of Napoleon, was himself known as the "Napoleon of Commerce"; his office was patterned on Napoleon's Empire room from the Palace at Compiegne.

Continue walking downtown on Broadway to:

"A growing city built on a narrow peninsula is unable to expand laterally, and must, therefore, soar. The problem was how to make it soar with dignity, and the problem has been solved . . ."
—From a 1921 article in *The Times* of London praising the Woolworth Building

8. **St. Paul's Chapel,** between Vesey and Fulton Streets. During the two years that New York was the nation's capital, George Washington worshiped at this 1766 Georgian chapel of Trinity Church. His pew is on one side of the church, the governor's on the opposite side. Charles Pierre L'Enfant (who laid out the city of Washington, D.C.) created the gilded sunburst above the altar. This is the city's only extant pre-Revolutionary church. Designed by Thomas McBean, with a temple-like portico and fluted Ionic columns supporting a massive pediment, it resembles London's St. Martin's-in-the-Fields. Under the east portico is a monument, erected in 1789, to General Richard Montgomery, one of the first Revolutionary patriots to die in battle. Prior to landfill, the Hudson used to flow next to St. Paul's, which must have been very picturesque. Do explore the small graveyard where 18th- and early-19th-century notables are buried. Chamber music and orchestral concerts are held here at noon most Mondays and Thursdays. Call 602-0747 for details.

Just downtown from St. Paul's stands the:

9. **A T & T Building,** at 195 Broadway. This early-20th-century (1915–22) neoclassic telecommunications tower has more exterior columns than any other building in the world. The 25-story structure rests on a Doric colonnade, with Ionic colonnades above, and the massively columned lobby evokes a Greek temple. The building's tower crown is modeled on the Mausoleum of Halicarnassus, one of the great Greek monuments of antiquity. Bronze panels over the entranceway by Paul Manship (sculptor of Rockefeller Center's Prometheus) symbolize wind, air, fire, and earth. No longer A T & T headquarters, the building is today the Kalikow Building.

Make a right on Dey Street. Up ahead—you can't miss it—is the:

10. **World Trade Center,** bounded by Vesey, West, Liberty, and Church Streets and best known for its famous 110-story twin towers. Still intact despite a terrorist bombing in early 1993, the WTC (opened in 1970 under the auspices of the Port Authority) comprises an immense complex. Its 12 million square feet of rentable office space house more than

350 firms and organizations. About 50,000 people work in its precincts, and some 70,000 others (tourists and businesspeople) visit them each day. The complex occupies 16 acres and includes, in addition to the towers, the sleek 22-story Vista Hotel, a plaza the size of four football fields (used for concerts, picnicking, and special events), an underground shopping mall, and several restaurants, most notably the spectacular Windows on the World (which will re-open in December 1995 after a major renovation).

The thing to do, of course, is whiz up to the 107th-floor Observation Deck to see the city from a 1,377-foot perspective. From there, be sure to ascend to the 110th-floor rooftop promenade—the world's highest open-air viewing platform—for even more magnificent views. Observation Deck facilities are open daily from 9:30am to 9:30pm (11:30pm in summer); tickets can be purchased on the mezzanine level of Two World Trade Center, where, by the way, you'll also find a TKTS booth should you want to obtain half-price theater tickets. Note, too, the artwork on the plaza by Alexander Calder, Louise Nevelson, Joan Miró, and others.

Take a Break   To optimally enjoy those 107th-floor views, consider dining "a quarter mile high in the sky" at **Windows on the World,** One World Trade Center (tel. 938-1100). At this writing Windows has not yet re-opened following the bombing of the World Trade Center a few years back, but renovation is in progress. Public relations people tell me that the fare will be international, the wine list excellent, and every table will afford a panoramic view. Prices will be on the high side. Call for reservations and further information.

For a quick meal, there's a snack bar on the **107th-floor observation deck of the World Trade Center.** And in summer there are outdoor cafés with tables under trees and umbrellas on the plaza as well, including a food court.

A delightful place for lunch is the **Greenhouse Café** in the Vista Hotel (tel. 444-4010), with an elegant conservatory ambience created by a lofty skylight ceiling, a windowed wall, and food displays under a gazebo. Trees in large planters thrive in the sunlight. Glance up, and you'll see the twin towers soaring overhead. A moderately priced cold buffet brunch here—a sumptuous spread including smoked fish, poached salmon, pâtés, beautiful salads, cheeses, fresh baked breads, and soup—is offered Monday through Saturday from 11:30am to 3pm, along with a pricier hot and cold buffet and an à la carte menu, the latter offered through 5pm. Sunday brunch (same hours) is a more elaborate affair, complete with champagne (it costs about $30). An excellent wine list is a Greenhouse Café plus. There's an entrance to the Vista off World Trade Center Plaza right between the twin towers.

The Vista also houses the nautically themed oak- and mahogany-paneled **Tall Ships Bar & Grill** (tel. 938-9100), on the lobby level, which serves lunch weekdays only from 11:30am to 2:30pm.

Entrées here run the gamut from fancy bar fare—a basket of fish and chips with garlic herb mayonnaise—to blackened swordfish steak with rosemary butter, grilled vegetables, and steamed potatoes. Prices are high to moderate.

Finally, you might explore the dining choices in varied price ranges—everything from pub fare to gourmet pizzas—at the World Financial Center (next listing). These are especially nice in good weather when you can dine al fresco at café tables overlooking the yacht basin.

Across the West Side Highway but reachable via an indoor walkway from the WTC is the:

11. **World Financial Center,** a dramatic office complex centered on the enormous glass-enclosed Winter Garden—a barrel-vaulted "crystal palace" filled with towering palms, each over 60 feet tall. Adjoining arcades house about 50 shops and restaurants, and a beautifully landscaped esplanade overlooks a yacht basin. An ongoing schedule of events, concerts, and exhibits takes place here—everything from jazz concerts to photography shows. Call 945-0505 to find out what's on during your visit.

Walk back to Church Street, make a left on Liberty Street to Broadway, and continue downtown a couple of blocks to:

12. **Trinity Church,** Broadway and Wall Street. Serving God and Mammon, this Wall Street house of worship—with

Gothic flying buttresses, beautiful stained-glass windows, and vaulted ceilings—was designed by Richard Upjohn and consecrated on Ascension Day in 1846. At that time its soaring spire, crested by a gilded cross, dominated the skyline. Its main doors, embellished with biblical scenes, are modeled after Ghiberti's famed doors of Florence's Baptistery.

The original church on this site went up in 1697 and burned down in 1776 during the Revolution. This first structure was just outside a massive wall marking the boundaries of the Dutch settlement—hence the name Wall Street. In the churchyard, where the oldest grave dates to 1681, are the burial sites of steamboat inventor Robert Fulton, Alexander Hamilton, and Captain James Lawrence, whose famous last words were "Don't give up the ship." You can pick up a graveyard map on the premises. A brief lecture tour is given weekdays at 2pm. There's also a small historical museum on the premises displaying documents, burial records, photographs, diary excerpts, communion platters, and other items, most of them interpretive of the relationship between the church and the city. Also on display here are replicas of the pistols used during the duel between Alexander Hamilton and Aaron Burr. Note the founding charter of Trinity Parish, granted by King William III of England in 1697, at the museum's entrance.

Make a left into Wall Street and walk one block to the:

13. **Federal Hall National Memorial,** 26 Wall Street at Nassau Street. Fronted by 32-foot fluted marble Doric columns, this imposing 1842 Greek Revival building is largely famous for the history of an earlier building that stood on the site. There Peter Zenger, publisher of the outspoken *Weekly Journal,* stood trial in 1735 for "seditious libel" against Royal Governor William Cosby. Specific issues of the paper, which had printed anti-Cosby songs, were burned in front of City Hall, and Zenger spent nine months in jail awaiting trial. His eventual acquittal set the precedent for freedom of the press, later guaranteed in the Bill of Rights. Congress met here after the Revolution, when New York was briefly the nation's capital. An 1883 statue of George Washington on the steps commemorates his inauguration at this site in 1789. And it was in Federal Hall, by the way,

on June 26, 1775, that General Washington made one of his most noted speeches to New Yorkers who feared the establishment of a military government: "When we assumed the soldier," he said, "we did not lay aside the citizen; and we shall most sincerely rejoice with you in that happy hour when the establishment of American liberty, upon the most firm and solid foundations, shall enable us to return to our private stations in the bosom of a free, peaceful, and happy country." Exhibits within elucidate these events along with other aspects of American history. Admission is free.

Cross Wall Street, where Nassau changes to Broad Street, and head to the Visitors' Center entrance of the:

14. **New York Stock Exchange,** which came into being in 1792 for the purpose of selling government bonds to pay Revolutionary War debts. Today, America's financial nerve center is housed in this 1903 Corinthian-columned Beaux Arts "temple" with an allegorical pediment sculpture by John Quincy Adams Ward depicting *Integrity Protecting the Works of Man* (Michael Milken take note). The original marble figures of this pediment, having deteriorated, were replaced by lead-coated copper replicas in 1936. Close to 2,500 companies are listed on the exchange; they have a combined value of about $4.5 trillion!

On self-guided tours weekdays between 9:15am and 4pm (the last tour leaves at 3:15pm), you can learn all about stock trading, view exhibits and a short film on the history and workings of the stock market, and watch the frenzied action on the trading floor. The observation platform has been glassed in since the 1960s when Abbie Hoffman and Jerry Rubin created chaos by tossing dollar bills onto the exchange floor. Ticket distribution, on a first-come, first-served basis, begins at 9am. There's no charge for the tour.

To reach Fraunces Tavern continue south on Broad Street to Pearl Street, a historic block lined with 18th- and 19th-century buildings.

Winding Down **Fraunces Tavern,** 54 Pearl Street (tel. 269-0144), is listed as a place to eat, but it's also a legitimate stop on the tour (see box). The two upper stories house the Fraunces Tavern Museum, where you can

Samuel Fraunces and George Washington

Throughout most of 17th-century Nieuw Amsterdam, the landfill upon which Fraunces Tavern is situated did not exist. It wasn't until the beginning of the 18th century that Mayor Stephanus Van Cortlandt bought a "water lot" at the site and filled it in for his daughter, Anne, and son-in-law, Stephen Delancey, who built a magnificent three-story Georgian mansion here in 1719.

In 1762 it was reincarnated as the Queen's Head Tavern, which owner Samuel Fraunces advertised as an establishment that entertained "Gentlemen, Ladies, and others [whatever that means] in the most genteel and convenient manner." Its name notwithstanding, in the 1770s, the Queen's Head became a meeting place for revolutionary patriots, though Fraunces also retained the patronage of Tory leaders. During the Revolution, he passed valuable information about troop movements gleaned from the latter on to General Washington, who later praised him for maintaining "a constant Friendship and attention to the Cause of our Country and its Independence and Freedom."

Here, in 1783, New York Governor George Clinton held a dinner for George Washington to celebrate America's victory and the evacuation of the British. A month later Washington bid a sentimental farewell to his officers in the long room: "With a heart full of love and gratitude, I now take leave of you. I most devoutly wish that your latter days may be as prosperous and happy as your former ones have been glorious and honorable." The Revolution won, Fraunces renamed the tavern for himself. After 1789 Fraunces went to work for Washington as his household steward. During the 19th century, the building suffered the ravages of several fires. In 1904, the Sons of the Revolution purchased and restored it based on typical period buildings rather than exact specifications.

view the room in which Washington's historic farewell took place (today set up to represent a typical 18th-century tavern room) and see other American history exhibits. A small admission is charged. Hours are Monday through Friday from 10am to 4:45pm and Saturdays from noon to 4pm.

The main floor today contains a very charming oak-paneled dining room with a working fireplace. Tables are set with pewter plates. The menu features steaks, seafood, pasta dishes, and colonial fare such as Yankee pot roast. A good buy here is a three-course prix-fixe lunch for $17.76. Or you can opt for pub fare in the more moderately priced Tap Room, which has plush burgundy leather furnishings and walls hung with historic American flags and hunting trophies. Reservations are suggested at both; better yet, arrive off hours to avoid crowds. The restaurant is open weekdays for breakfast from 7 to 10am and for lunch from 11:30am to 4pm; the Tap Room is open daily from 11:30am to closing.

CHINATOWN

Start: The intersection of Broadway and Canal Street.

Subway: Take the 6, N, R, J, M, or Z to Canal Street.

Finish: The intersection of East Broadway and Rutgers Street.

Time: 3 to 4 hours, not including restaurant stops.

Best Time: Any time the weather is conducive to walking.

Everyone comes to Chinatown for the food; the neighborhood's four-hundred-odd restaurants have for many years been satisfying New Yorkers' cravings for Cantonese, Hunan, and Szechuan fare, as well as Thai and Vietnamese cuisines. But outside the doors of the restaurants waits the swirling, exotic streetlife of one of the largest Chinese communities in the Western Hemisphere. In the shops along Mott, Canal, and East Broadway, you'll find unusual foodstuffs, Chinese herbal medicines, and collectibles that you'd think only a trip to Hong Kong or Shanghai could net. And you can also uncover in Chinatown's narrow streets and aging tenements the legacies of immigrants—first the English, then the Germans, Irish, Italians, Jews, and finally the Chinese—who have made this neighborhood one of their first stops in the New World.

Although East Indies trading ships brought handfuls of Chinese to New York from about 1840 on, it was not until the 1880s that Chinatown really began to develop. Thousands of

Chinese sailed to California (they called it *Gam San,* the "Gold Mountain") in the mid–19th century, hoping to amass fortunes by working the mines and building railroads, so they could return to China rich men. They were willing to work long hours for low pay, and most had little interest in learning English and assimilating American culture. By the 1870s, they became the victims of a tide of racism, violence, and legal persecution throughout the West. In 1882, Congress passed the Chinese Exclusion Act, which denied Chinese the right to citizenship, barred them from all but a handful of occupations, and suspended the immigration of Chinese laborers to the United States. Additionally, the act forbade any laborers already in the country from bringing their wives here. Some Chinese returned home, but tens of thousands remained and many drifted east to escape the hostile climate in the West. From 1880 to 1890 the Chinese population on Mott, Pell, and Doyers Streets increased tenfold to 12,000.

By the 1890s, Chinatown had become a large and isolated ghetto, and remained so for many years. Since World War II, however, the neighborhood has been building bridges to the American mainstream. A large influx of foreign capital from Taiwan and Hong Kong has helped make Chinatown one of New York's strongest local economies, and many Chinese Americans have joined the middle class. Come to Chinatown on a Sunday and you'll do your exploring alongside well-heeled suburbanites in for a look at the old neighborhood. But unlike other famous immigrant neighborhoods such as Little Italy or the old Lower East Side, Chinatown isn't ready to be relegated to the history books—immigrants from all around Asia continue to stream in, adding new energy and color.

● ● ● ● ● ● ● ● ● ● ● ● ● ● ● ●

Set off to the east along Canal Street. You'll probably have to thread your way through a multiethnic throng of pedestrians and street vendors hawking toys, firecrackers, dumplings, and the like—Canal Street during business hours is one of New York's most frenzied, crowded thoroughfares. From Broadway to the Bowery, Canal Street (which is a major east-west conduit for traffic from Brooklyn over the Manhattan Bridge to New Jersey through the Holland Tunnel) is lined with bustling variety stores, fish markets, green grocers, banks, and Chinese-owned jewelry shops. Many of the storefronts have been subdivided into minimalls whose stalls purvey everything from ginseng products to martial arts paraphernalia. When night falls and the shops are shuttered, Canal Street quickly becomes almost completely deserted. Although you'll see plenty of Chinese-language signs on Canal as soon as you walk east of Broadway, the landmark that signals your arrival in Chinatown proper is the former:

1. **Golden Pacific National Bank.** Located on the northwest corner of Canal and Centre Streets, this building was raised in 1983 as the bank's new home. At first a major point of pride in the neighborhood, the bank failed only two years later and its patrons, largely individual Chinese, lost their uninsured deposits. Its colorful building, with a jade-trimmed red pagoda roof and an elaborately decorated facade with Oriental phoenix and dragon motifs, has been resurrected as a busy jewelry exchange. Walk around on Centre Street to see the building in its entirety.

Continue east along Canal Street, and look for a group of vegetable sellers plying their trade on a traffic island at Baxter Street. Here you can peruse and purchase authentic Chinese produce—bok choy (delicate Chinese cabbage, delicious when stir-fried), small white and red-violet eggplants, taro root, fresh ginger, Chinese squash, big white winter melons with pulpy centers, tender bamboo shoots, yard-long green beans, pale golden lily buds, lotus leaves, cucumber-sized okras, turnips resembling large white horseradish, and sweet snow peas. Cross from the traffic island to the southern side of Canal Street where you'll smell a briny aroma emanating from a fish market (no. 214) whose crushed-ice–covered offerings spill well out onto the sidewalk. The aproned fish sellers keep up a steady patter, extolling the virtues of their shark, squid, snapper, oysters, and eels. Here and throughout your tour, you'll also pass carts vending Peking duck, chicken feet, roast pork, and lo mein, and store windows displaying barbecued chickens, ducks, and squab with heads and beaks fully intact.

On the southwest corner of Canal Street and the Bowery (at 58 Bowery) is a branch of the:

Dim Sum: A Chinatown Tradition

Dim sum is Cantonese for "dot your heart," and a dim sum meal consists of one small gastronomic delight after another. Simply choose what looks appealing from the steaming carts that servers wheel around to your table. Dim sum usually involves over 100 appetizer-sized items—perhaps crystal shrimp dumplings, steamed leek dumplings, deep-fried minced shrimp rolls wrapped in bacon, steamed beef rolls in bean curd skins, sweet doughy buns filled with tangy morsels of barbecued pork, deep-fried shrimp, beef ribs with black pepper sauce, honey roast pork rolled in steamed noodles, and much more. There are dessert dim sum as well, such as orange pudding, egg custard rolls covered with shredded coconut, and sweet lotus-seed sesame balls.

2. **Republic Bank for Savings.** Built in 1924, and later overhauled and tailored to its Chinese depositors, this dome-roofed bank is one of New York's most distinctive. Its name is inscribed in Chinese over its main portal, and its interior is decorated with several dozen beautiful framed Ching dynasty paintings, some of them displayed in carved and gilded rosewood screens. A red and gold pagoda structure houses the bank's coffers, and the walls are lined with Chinese proverbs, which translate to: "Wealth comes from saving your money," "When you have money, you can do whatever you like," and "If you're filthy rich, you're born with it; moderate wealth requires hard work." Other panels wish depositors good luck and advise thoughtful consideration for others. The domed ceiling is unfortunately obscured by a very unaesthetic fluorescent lighting system.

Canal Street is lined with one bank after another; indeed Chinatown's 161,000 residents are served by several dozen banks—more than most cities of similar size. Many Chinatown residents routinely put away 30% to 50% of their wages.

Across the Bowery to the east is the approach to the:

3. **Manhattan Bridge.** This suspension bridge, built in 1905, may not be the inspiration to poets and artists that the great Brooklyn Bridge has been, but the monumental Beaux Arts colonnade and arch that stand at its entrance (in odd juxtaposition to the functional steel towers of the bridge) are quite grand and arresting.

    Looming above the bridge on the east side of the Bowery is:

4. **Confucius Plaza.** The first major public-funded housing project built for Chinese use, Confucius Plaza extends from Division Street around to the Bowery where it rises up into a curved 43-story tower facing the entrance to the Manhattan Bridge.

    The activist spirit of the 1960s touched Chinatown in a significant way; many neighborhood youths became involved in a Chinese-American pride movement that culminated in the establishment of new organizations devoted to building community centers, providing social services, and securing Chinatown a voice in city government. Winning the struggle to build Confucius Plaza and forcing contractors to hire Chinese workers showed that Chinatown was now a political heavy hitter.

    Walk south on the Bowery to no. 18, at the southeast corner of the Bowery and Pell Street, to the:

5. **Edward Mooney House,** (occupied by Summit Mortgage Bankers). This largely Georgian brick row house (painted dark plum with beige trim) dates from George Washington's New York days. It was built in 1785 and is the oldest such house in the city. Mooney was a wealthy meat wholesaler who snapped up this property after prominent New York Tory James De Lancey abandoned it—and the new nation—after the Revolutionary War.

    The Bowery reaches its southern terminus in Chatham Square, into which nine other streets converge. To your left on a traffic island you'll see the:

6. **Statue of Confucius.** Built in 1976 to complement the Confucius Plaza development, this bronze statue and its green marble base were a gift of the Chinese Consolidated Benevolent Association (CCBA), which has served as Chinatown's unofficial government for over a hundred years.

Chinatown

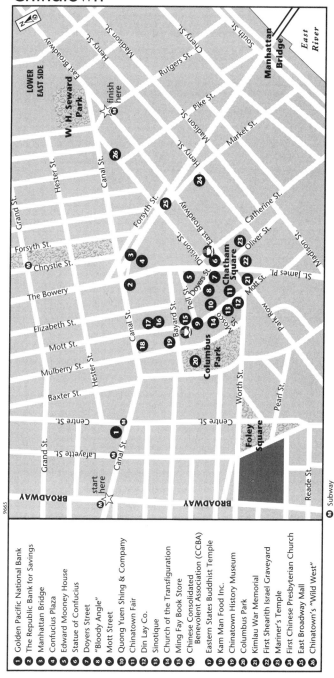

1. Golden Pacific National Bank
2. The Republic Bank for Savings
3. Manhattan Bridge
4. Confucius Plaza
5. Edward Mooney House
6. Statue of Confucius
7. Doyers Street
8. "Bloody Angle"
9. Mott Street
10. Quong Yuen Shing & Company
11. Chinatown Fair
12. Din Lay Co.
13. Sinotique
14. Church of the Transfiguration
15. Ming Fay Book Store
16. Chinese Consolidated Benevolent Association (CCBA)
17. Eastern States Buddhist Temple
18. Kam Man Food Inc.
19. Chinatown History Museum
20. Columbus Park
21. Kimlau War Memorial
22. First Shearith Israel Graveyard
23. Mariner's Temple
24. First Chinese Presbyterian Church
25. East Broadway Mall
26. Chinatown's "Wild West"

Ⓜ Subway

The organization has always represented conservative Chinese who support traditional notions of family loyalty and respect for one's elders and leaders; the statue was built over the strenuous objections of activist groups that felt the neighborhood should display a more progressive cultural symbol. However, the sage's 2,400-year-old words, inscribed in the monument's base in both Chinese and English, are strikingly descriptive of the strength of Chinatown's tight-knit social fabric: Confucius recommends that we look beyond our immediate family and see *all* our elders as our parents, and all children as our own.

From the statue of Confucius, follow Catherine Street past the pagoda-roofed Republic Bank for Savings, then turn left onto East Broadway. This thoroughfare is now the heart of commercial, workaday Chinatown. Very few of its businesses are oriented toward tourists; instead, they are dedicated to serving the Chinese community's needs. There are Chinese video stores, beauty salons, sidewalk shacks purveying grilled meats and dumplings, and bakeries whose wedding cakes are topped with Asian bride and groom figurines.

Take a Break For lunch, treat yourself to a dim sum meal. Every day from 8am to about 4pm, two huge, showy restaurants—the **Golden Unicorn** at 18 East Broadway (tel. 941-0911) and the **Nice Restaurant** at 35 East Broadway (tel. 406-9510)—draw large, hungry crowds. The Golden Unicorn's walkie-talkie–wielding hostess directs incoming diners to the restaurant's second- and third-floor dining rooms, whereas in the Nice Restaurant, the lobby has several tanks full of carp and sea bass. Usually you'll be seated with other parties around a huge banquet table. Once you're settled, you'll see that there's a distinctly celebratory spirit pervading these swank dining rooms; the Chinese families dining here often seem to have three or four generations represented when they go out for a meal. Help yourself—you can afford to take some risks since everything costs just $2 to $4 (prices at Nice are a tad lower than Golden Unicorn's) but don't grab anything unless it really appeals to you. Though servers seldom speak much English, fellow Chinese diners at your table are usually helpful.

Backtrack to Chatham Square. At the Bowery, on the square, a narrow, crooked street bears off to the northwest. This is:

7. **Doyers Street,** which along with Pell Street and the lower end of Mott Street formed the original Chinatown. Doyers was the backdrop for much of the neighborhood's unhappy early history.

Chinatown's "bachelor society," which existed from 1882 to 1943 (when some provisions of the Exclusion Act were repealed), was a place of grimly limited opportunity and deep poverty. There were 27 men to every woman in the neighborhood. Prohibited from competing with whites for work—and hemmed into Chinatown by the language barrier and even the risk of being beaten if they strayed from the three-block ghetto—most of the men eked out a living in the laundry industry.

Crime compounded the neighborhood's misery. The Chinese moved into the northern end of an area that for 40 years had been a sprawling morass of saloons, gambling dens, and squalid tenements extending from Chatham Square all the way to the waterfront. Prostitution flourished (out of desperation many Chinese men lived with, or even married, white prostitutes) and opium dens sprang up. The Chinese Consolidated Benevolent Association (CCBA) acted as de facto government, but real power resided in the *tongs*—protection societies involved in racketeering and gambling. There are still tong-controlled gaming dens in Chinatown, still whispers of intimidation and an occasional outbreak of gang-related violence.

The post office located a few paces up Doyers Street on your right now occupies the site of the old Chatham Club, one of the uproarious music halls that surrounded Chatham Square a century ago. The clubs boasted singing waiters, accompanied by a tinny piano, who would entertain the clientele with sentimental ballads. Both Izzy Baline and Al Yoelson sang at the Chatham and other clubs on Doyers; in tonier surroundings, they later became better known as Irving Berlin and Al Jolson.

By the 1920s, the sharp bend in Doyers Street had acquired its reputation as the infamous:

Pulp Fiction

As lawless as "bachelor society" Chinatown could be, the reality always paled in comparison to the lurid portraits of the community retailed by the newspapers and tour guides. The most notorious of the tour guides was one Chuck Connors. A gifted storyteller, he translated his familiarity with the Cantonese dialect and his willingness to take license with the truth into celebrity among the New York socialites he would escort through the neighborhood. Connors never hesitated to point to any man walking down the street and label him a hatchetman for the tongs or an opium addict; his baroque finale was a fake opium den, complete with a man and woman posing as opium addict and "white slave girl." Such fictions satisfied the sensation-seekers of that time, but had little in common with the day-to-day existence of almost all of Chinatown's men.

8. **"Bloody Angle."** The first two tongs to rise in Chinatown, the On Leong and the Hip Sing, engaged in a fierce struggle for turf and precedence in Chinatown that dragged on for almost 40 years. Both organizations had large "standing armies" of henchmen, and the worst of the bloodshed between the two tongs occurred here. The crooked street lent itself to ambush, and assassins could usually make a fast escape by ducking through the old Chinese Theatre, which stood right in the elbow of the street, that the Viet-Nam restaurant now occupies. At the turn of the century, Bloody Angle was the site of more murders than anywhere else in the United States.

At the end of Doyers is Pell Street, another short, narrow thoroughfare lined with restaurants that has changed little over the years. At no. 16 is the unobtrusive entryway to the headquarters of the organization that has dominated Pell and Doyers Streets for a hundred years, the Hip Sing tong, its green and gold sign symbolizing growth and prosperity, respectively.

Leaving the dark side of the neighborhood's history behind, walk west on Pell to its intersection with:

9. **Mott Street,** the heart of old Chinatown. Mott is the epicenter of the tumultuous Chinese New Year celebrations that begin with the first full moon after January 21. For weeks beforehand, shops all through Chinatown do a booming business as residents stock up for their holiday feasts, purchase presents for friends and family, and buy New Year's bells, firecrackers, lucky lotus seeds and birds, and calendars. Red and gold streamers festoon every shop window and interior, hang over every street, and brighten every home at New Year's. When the big day arrives, one of New York's most chaotic and colorful street parties begins, featuring parades complete with gyrating dragon dancers and a nonstop thunder of firecrackers.

The shops that line Mott Street are a diverse bunch, and collectively their stock will surely give you the chance to bring a piece of Chinatown back home with you. Just around the corner to your left is one such store:

10. **Quong Yuen Shing & Company,** at 32 Mott Street. The oldest store in Chinatown, Quong Yuen Shing celebrated its 100th birthday in 1991. It has changed remarkably little—the tin ceiling, hanging scales, and the decorative panels in the back above the ornately framed counter (over which Chinese herbal medicines were once dispensed) all keep the place looking just as it did in the 1890s. Along with sandalwood fans, tea and mah-jongg sets, various ceramic bowls and vases, and seeds for all those Chinese vegetables on sale in the streets, the store still sells merchandise it's been stocking for a century. One such item are silk handkerchiefs, which Chinatown laundries would buy and pass on to their best customers at Christmastime.

Make your way down to the:

11. **Chinatown Fair,** at 8 Mott Street. Tucked in between the familiar video game machines here are vintage pinball games and other arcade antiques like the Luv-O-Meter, the test-your-strength machine, and a photobooth. Two glass-enclosed booths house live performing chickens—one is a master of tic-tac-toe (you win a large bag of fortune cookies if you beat her) and the other dances. A sign above the dancer's booth advises that how well she performs "depends on her mood."

Across Mott is the:

12. **Din Lay Co.,** at 5 Mott Street. An old, slightly musty shop, Din Lay is worth a visit for its unbeatable collection of classic Chinatown souvenirs—there are mah-jongg sets and tables, incense burners, joss sticks, tea sets, delicate rice-paper fans and stationery, sandalwood-scented soap, stainless-steel balls to roll in your hand to improve your strength and coordination, and much more.

A few doors up to the north is:

13. **Sinotique,** at 19a Mott Street. Inside this refined, decidedly upscale shop you'll find beautiful, high-quality Chinese antiques, crafts, and collectibles. On a recent visit, these included rosewood and teak cabinets with delicate hand-carved ornamentation; pottery ranging from unglazed pieces created in the 2nd millenium B.C. through the Ching Dynasty, as well as Sung Dynasty celadon porcelains; exquisite carved bamboo birdcages from southern China; Chinese country furniture; Tibetan, Chinese, and Mongolian rugs; 19th-century Chinese watercolors, hand-wrought mounted bronze gongs and jewelry. New Age and classical Chinese music (the CDs are sold here) creates a peaceful backdrop to this incense-scented emporium, and chimes ring gently in the doorway as you enter and exit.

Cross tiny Mosco Street (named for a prominent Little Italy politician), and you'll be in front of the:

14. **Church of the Transfiguration,** at 25–29 Mott Street. This Georgian stone church, with a number of traceried Gothic windows, was built in 1801; the spire was added in the 1860s. Originally consecrated as the English Lutheran First Church of Zion, Transfiguration has remade itself in the changing image of the neighborhood many times, first as a house of worship for English Lutherans, and then, after it was reconsecrated as a Catholic church, serving the newly arrived Irish, and later, in the 1880s, the Italians. You can still hear an English mass at Transfiguration, but nowadays its Cantonese and Mandarin services draw far greater crowds—the church is the focal point of New York's Chinese Roman Catholic community. Transfiguration remains true to its heritage as a mission house, continuing to offer English classes and other services that help its members find their way into the American mainstream.

☕ **Take a Break** Just beyond Pell Street is the **New Lung Fong Bakery,** 41 Mott Street (tel. 233-7447), offering an array of sweet treats such as red-bean cakes, black-bean doughnuts, custard tarts, chestnut buns, cream buns, melon cakes, and mixed-nut pies. Sitting in Lung Fong's unadorned café section, you can relax with a cup of tea or very good coffee and *yum cha*—that's Chinese for hanging out, talking and drinking, in a café. All of Lung Fong's pastry is marked with English labels.

Continue walking north on Mott. Across the street at 42 Mott Street is the:

15. **Ming Fay Book Store.** An eclectic store stocked with everything from art/school supplies and toys to Chinese calendars, newspapers, comics, pinup magazines, and books, Ming Fay also carries an interesting selection of English-language books on Chinese subjects. A sampling of titles: *Chinese Astrology, The Bruce Lee Story, Chinese Idioms, The Dictionary of Traditional Chinese Medicine,* and *The Living Buddha.*

Just past the bookstore is a permanent food stall that sells nothing but fried white-radish cakes, and a little farther up Mott at no. 62 is the headquarters of the:

16. **Chinese Consolidated Benevolent Association (CCBA).** Until fairly recently, it functioned as the working government of Chinatown, helping new immigrants find jobs and housing, funneling capital into neighborhood businesses, offering English classes to children and adults, providing services to the elderly, and even operating criminal courts. While its influence has waned somewhat, it is still a major social and political force in Chinatown, and is the voice of New York's pro-Taiwan community. Also located in the building is the Chinese School, which since 1915 has been working to keep the Chinese traditions and language alive, long a primary concern of the CCBA.

Right next door is the:

17. **Eastern States Buddhist Temple of America.** This storefront shrine has been here for years. Quiet and suffused with incense, it serves as something of a social center; there are usually a number of elderly ladies sitting in the

chairs and benches that line the wall. Enter, light a joss stick, and offer a prayer to Kuan Yin, the Chinese goddess of mercy. Or perhaps you'd rather supplicate the Four-Faced Buddha for good luck in business (money will come from all directions, hence the four faces). You can also buy a fortune here, in English, for a dollar—a shameless pandering to tourism, but, nevertheless, rather fun. Mine said:

> *Probability of success: excellent.*
> *There is a tower of good height,*
> *It gives out a guiding beacon light,*
> *As you have fought a stalwart fight,*
> *Success brings you much more delight.*

Across the street at the corner of Mott and Canal (83–85 Mott), behind a stately facade that includes balconies and a pagoda roof, is the headquarters of the Chinese Merchants Association, better known as On Leong. This is Chinatown's oldest tong and still one of its most prominent neighborhood organizations.

Make a left onto Canal Street, where a steady stream of shoppers will no doubt be passing in and out of:

18. **Kam Man Food Inc.** at 200 Canal Street. The *ne plus ultra* of Chinese supermarkets, Kam Man makes for a truly fascinating browse. To your right as you enter the store is a selection of elaborately packaged teas and elixirs laced with ginseng and other mainstays of Chinese pharmacopoeia. These include items such as tzepao sanpien extract (which promises greater potency to men), heart tonics, stopsmoking and slimming teas, deer-tail extract, edible bird's nests, tiger liniment, and royal jelly. Many, such as bu tian su—good for memory loss, insomnia, an aching back, or lumbago, among other things—claim to cure a wide variety of ailments. Just beyond this collection is a counter displaying myriad varieties of ginseng. Walk toward the rear of the store and you'll find packages of pork buns ready for the steamer, quail eggs, dried seafood (oysters, shrimps, mussels, anchovies), exotic dried mushrooms and other funghi, sauces ranging from oyster to black-bean garlic, salted duck eggs, meats (there's an entire butcher section), frozen Chinese vegetables, and much more. Downstairs there are teas,

kitchenware and cookery items from woks to tea sets, fancy chopsticks, sweets like preserved plums and tamarind candy, roasted seaweed, and oodles of noodles. And shelves on the landing between floors are stocked with healing teas and health beverages; pick up some essence of tienchi flowers, a purported remedy for pimples, dizziness, hot temper, grinding of teeth, and emotional inquietude. After a few minutes at Kam Man, all the Chinese unrecognizables become the norm, and it's the odd jar of mayonnaise or box of baking powder that really looks strange.

Turn left onto Mulberry Street (another thoroughfare lined with emporia that make for great browsing and window shopping), to visit the:

19. **Chinatown History Museum,** 70 Mulberry Street (second floor, entrance on Bayard Street, tel. 619-4785). In the forward-looking, upwardly mobile climate of today's Chinatown, not many want to think about the cruel hardships that the first generations of Chinese in New York suffered. This museum, founded in 1980, documents with changing exhibits the history and culture of Chinese in America from the early 1800s to the present. An adjoining gallery stages exhibitions of works by Chinese artists and photographers, and there's a gift/book store on the premises. Hours are Sunday through Friday from noon to 5pm; a small admission is charged.

Opening off to the southwest on the other side of Mulberry Street is:

20. **Columbus Park.** Open public spaces are in short supply on the Lower East Side of Manhattan, and Columbus Park is popular with Chinatown residents both young and old. Here old Chinese women play cards or have their fortunes told, while, in another area, Chinese men gamble over checkers. The park lies where a huddle of decrepit tenements known as Mulberry Bend once stood. In the last quarter of the 19th century, Mulberry Bend was New York's very worst slum, as evinced by the frightening nomenclature it acquired—the filthy rookeries went by names such as Bone Alley, Kerosene Row, and Bandits' Roost. Such brawling street gangs as the Dead Rabbits, Plug Uglies, and Whyos were the powers of Mulberry Bend, and police would only

venture into the area in platoons of 10 or more. Mulberry Bend remained New York's disgrace until social reformer Jacob Riis managed to work public ire up to the point where city officials were obliged to raze the slum between 1892 and 1894. For the last century, Riis's vision of a clean place for neighborhood children to play has been made a reality—there's a big playground and games of basketball, baseball, or hockey are almost always in progress.

At the southern end of the park, make a left turn onto Worth Street and you'll soon be back at Chatham Square. Up ahead on your right on the traffic island is the:

21. **Kimlau War Memorial,** built in 1962 to honor the Chinese Americans who gave their lives while serving in the U.S. armed forces. Chinatown's extraordinary contribution to the American war effort in World War II—40% of the neighborhood's population served in the military—was a major factor in the annulment of the Chinese Exclusion Act and other anti-Chinese legislation.

St. James Place, which extends south from Chatham Square, is the site of the:

22. **First Shearith Israel Graveyard,** a burial ground for the Sephardic Jews who emigrated to New York in the mid–17th century. The 1683 stone of Benjamin Bueno de Mesquita (still legible) is the oldest in the city; the cemetery remained active until 1828 and features the graves of a number of soldiers who died during the American Revolution. Also buried here, in 1733, is Rachel Rodriguez Marques, an ancestor of Bernard Baruch; thus Baruch paid for the improvement of the site in the 1950s.

Backtrack on St. James Place, and turn right onto Oliver Street. On the northeast corner of Oliver and Henry Streets is the:

23. **Mariner's Temple.** This Greek Revival brownstone church, with a portico entranceway fronted by two massive Ionic columns, was built in 1844. Today a Baptist church serving a mixed Chinese, African-American, and Latino congregation, the Mariner's Temple originally catered to the sea captains, dockworkers, and sailors of the sprawling maritime community that dominated the waterfront along the East River in the 19th century.

Two blocks east, on the corner of Henry and Market Streets, is the:

24. **First Chinese Presbyterian Church,** which shares a place in neighborhood history with the Mariner's Temple. Built in 1819 on the outskirts of the Cherry Hill section (which after the Revolutionary War was New York's poshest neighborhood and the site of the nation's first presidential mansion), this Georgian-style house of worship was originally named the Northeast Dutch Reformed Church. It was renamed the Church of Sea and Land during the mid-19th century, when the East River waterfront had become rife with cutthroat saloons, dance halls, and "crimps"—lodging houses that often took advantage of their sailor patrons by robbing them or even "shanghaiing" them aboard outgoing ships. Mission houses like the Mariner's Temple and the Church of Sea and Land were often the only place to which beleaguered seafarers and immigrants could turn for help. Today, the church continues to assist the immigrants who arrive in Chinatown in droves every year.

Turn left and follow Market Street to bustling East Broadway. As unlikely as this may seem, the dim, noisy area underneath the Manhattan Bridge is a commercial hot spot of Chinatown. You'll see on your left the:

25. **East Broadway Mall,** a place that may cause you to wonder if you're actually in Hong Kong. The stores cater entirely to Chinese shoppers and include a newsstand at which you'll be lucky to spot a word of English, a shop selling Chinese pop music, two Chinese-language video stores, several beauty salons and cosmetics shops selling products you won't find in your average health and beauty aids store, and Ho's Ginseng Co., where you can get something to cool down your blood (or warm it up). The mall's centerpiece is a glitzy upstairs restaurant, the Triple Eight Palace.

Continue along East Broadway, and you'll soon cross Pike Street. Pike is an unofficial divider between establishment Chinatown and an expanding area that's been termed:

26. **Chinatown's "Wild West"** by journalist Gwen Kinkead in her book *Chinatown: A Portrait of a Closed Society*

(HarperCollins, 1992). Asians have been flooding into New York City ever since U.S. immigration laws were liberalized in 1965. The great majority of them hail from the People's Republic of China, and most of these new immigrants come from Fujian Province, often via Hong Kong or Taiwan. These new arrivals have almost completely replaced the old immigrant residents of the Lower East Side, the Jews. Emblematic of the changing makeup in the neighborhood is the **Sons of Israel Kalwarie Synagogue,** located on Pike Street to the right of East Broadway. It now stands abandoned and boarded up like many of the Lower East Side's Jewish landmarks, sandwiched by Chinese stores.

Walk down East Broadway to Rutgers Street (where you'll find the entrance to the subway's East Broadway F-line stop). The Chinatown you'll pass on your way may have no fancy restaurants, curio shops, or pagoda roofs, but no storefront here stands empty. The barber shops, fish markets, and newsstands may look as though they've been built on a wing and a prayer, but they do a brisk business. Many of the buildings you pass house small garment factories just like the sweatshops in which Jewish laborers worked for their family's future on East Broadway 75 years ago. You'll find around you the hectic commerce, the hardworking laborers, the nearly dressed schoolchildren, the hum of a neighborhood whose people will soon be leaving these gritty tenement streets on their way into the mainstream, just as people on the Lower East Side have been doing for more than a century.

THE JEWISH LOWER EAST SIDE

Start: The Henry Street Settlement, 263–267 Henry Street.

Subway: Take the F train to East Broadway and Rutgers Street; walk south on Rutgers and make a left on Henry Street.

Finish: Russ and Daughters, 179 Houston Street.

Time: Approximately 5 to 6 hours if you do all the tours, and I highly recommend that you do.

Best Time: Sundays, when you can tour the Eldridge Street Synagogue (Stop 6) and see Orchard Street in full hubbub. If you begin about 9:30am, you'll also get a chance to look inside Bialystoker Synagogue (Stop 3). *Note:* Since tours of the highly recommended Lower East Side Tenement Museum sometimes fill up on Sundays, you might want to stop there earlier in the day (it opens at 11am) and pick up tickets; see details below (Stop 13).

Worst Time: Saturdays and Jewish holidays when almost everything is closed; Friday afternoons, when stores close early.

The Lower East Side has always been one of New York's most colorful neighborhoods. Over 23 million Europeans emigrated to American shores between 1880 and 1919, seeking escape from famine, poverty, and religious persecution. About 1.5 million Jews—many of them fleeing Russian pogroms—wound up in ramshackle tenements here. They scratched out a meager livelihood peddling wares on Orchard Street or working dawn to dusk in garment center sweatshops. By 1920, some five hundred synagogues and religious schools (talmud torahs) dotted the area. Though the garment center has moved uptown, and the ethnic mix is different today, Orchard Street—the area's primary shopping artery—and its immediate surroundings remain a largely Orthodox Jewish enclave. And the area is rich in Jewish history; 80% of today's American Jews are descendants of immigrants who once lived on these streets. Don't eat much before starting out; there's great noshing along the way.

• • • • • • • • • • • • • • • •

Our first stop is:

1. **The Henry Street Settlement,** 263–267 Henry Street. Called to tend a patient on Ludlow Street in 1892, 25-year-old German-Jewish nurse Lillian Wald was appalled at the squalor of tenement life. She moved downtown in order to study conditions in the Jewish ghetto, and, in 1893, established a district nursing service on Henry Street. Two years later, it evolved into the Henry Street Settlement, one of America's first social agencies, offering job training, educational facilities, activities and summer camps for children, concerts, and plays. German-Jewish philanthropist Jacob Schiff donated two of the three Henry Street buildings you see before you.

Wald dedicated her life to helping the indigent of the Lower East Side fight disease, malnutrition, and ignorance, and the "house on Henry Street" initiated progressive social legislation, including child labor laws. Social reformer Jacob Riis said of her, "From the very start, the poor became 'her people.' She took them to her heart and they quickly gave her unstinted love and trust . . ." Years ago you might have seen Jane Addams, Albert Einstein, or Eleanor Roosevelt discussing vital social issues in the dining room. More recently, President Bill Clinton visited during his 1992 campaign. The settlement continues its good works, operating homeless shelters and numerous other programs for neighborhood residents. Its three original (and beautifully restored) late-Federal buildings, today used only for administrative purposes, are designated landmarks—remnants of a once-affluent neighborhood.

Make a right on Montgomery Street, and bear right to Samuel Dickstein Place. Across Grand Street is:

2. **The Louis Abrons Arts Center/Harry De Jur Henry Street Settlement Playhouse,** 466 Grand Street. Founded by sisters Alice and Irene Lewisohn in 1915 to stage productions of the Henry Street Settlement's youthful dramatic groups, this renowned center went on to present premieres of S. Ansky's *The Dybbuk* (attended by authors Edna Ferber and Willa Cather) and James Joyce's *Exiles,* along with plays by George Bernard Shaw, Havelock Ellis, Anton Chekhov, Scholem Asch, and Eugene O'Neill. It remains a vital performance space and cultural center, offering a comprehensive schedule of dance, theater, music, art exhibits, classes, and workshops. Pick up an events schedule while you're here. The center is housed in a three-story Georgian Revival building with a newer adjacent extension.

Around the corner on Willett Street, to your left, is the:

3. **Bialystoker Synagogue,** 7 Bialystoker Place (Willett Street). Occupying a converted 1826 Federal-style fieldstone church with a pedimented facade, this beautiful Orthodox landsmanschaft shul (synagogue of countrymen) was purchased in 1905 by an immigrant congregation from Bialystok (then in Russia, today in Poland). The congregation itself was organized in 1878, and, in honor of its 100th anniversary, Willett Street was renamed Bialystoker Place in 1978. The temple's interior walls are ornately painted with Moorish motifs, zodiac signs (which are found in the Jewish scriptural interpretations of the cabala), and biblical scenes such as the Wailing Wall and the burial place of Rachel. The gold-leafed ark, designed in Italy, is embellished with cornucopias, crowns, lions, and eagles.

There are beautiful stained-glass windows, and glittering crystal chandeliers are suspended from a ceiling painted as a blue sky with fluffy white clouds. Go in via the downstairs steps, and take a good look around.

Bialystoker Synagogue is open on Sundays until about 10:30am (there are services from 6:15 to 10am); if you're going at another time, you can call a day or two ahead (tel. 475-0165) to arrange admission.

Return to Grand Street and make a right, then make a left on Clinton Street, and a right on East Broadway to the:

4. **Educational Alliance (the David Sarnoff Building),** 197 East Broadway. The Alliance was founded in 1889 by "uptown" German-Jewish philanthropists to help fellow immigrants assimilate, Americanize, and adapt to a baffling alien culture. It offered them training in English, courses in business, cultural and civic programs, legal counsel, music lessons, and athletic facilities, not to mention such hard-to-come-by amenities as hot showers and pasteurized milk for children. Here preschool youngsters attended enrichment programs to prepare them for public school, a forerunner of the Head Start program of the 1960s. Immigrants learned about American history, celebrated new holidays like July Fourth and Lincoln's birthday, and attended lectures on everything from American literature to philosophy.

Today, the Educational Alliance's programs operate out of 21 locations and serve not only Jews, but black, Chinese, and Latin American New Yorkers. A Hall of Fame on the main floor is lined with photos of notable alumni such as Eddie Cantor, David Sarnoff, Jan Peerce, Jacob Epstein, Arthur Murray, and Louise Nevelson.

Continue in the same direction to:

5. **The Forward Building,** 175 East Broadway. For 60 years, this was the home of America's most prominent Yiddish newspaper—one of over 150 such papers published around the turn of the century. Founded in 1897 by a group of Russian Jewish immigrants, the *"Forverts"* guided thousands of Eastern European Jews through the confusing maze of American society. In the 1920s, its circulation was 250,000 copies a day.

Lithuanian immigrant Abraham Cahan served as editor from the newspaper's inception until his death in 1951.

The Jewish Lower East Side

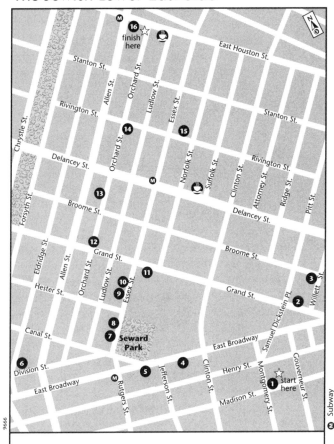

1. The Henry Street Settlement
2. The Louis Abrons Art Center/Harry De Jur Henry Street Settlement Playhouse
3. Bialystoker Synagogue
4. The Educational Alliance
5. The Forward Building
6. Eldridge Street Synagogue
7. The Bezalel Jewish Art Gallery
8. Weinfeld's Skull Cap Mfg.
9. Essex Street Pickles
10. Hebrew Religious Articles
11. Kossar's Bialys
12. Orchard Street
13. Lower East Side Tenement Museum
14. First Roumanian-American Congregation
15. Schapiro's Wine Company
16. Russ and Daughters

Under his inspired guidance, this socialist and zealously pro-labor newspaper examined every facet of Jewish and American life. It explained American customs and social graces to greenhorns—everything from baseball to personal hygiene—and exhorted readers to learn English and educate their children. Readers could air their problems in the New World in a column called the Bintel Brief (Bundle of Letters)—an immigrant version of Ann Landers. And the paper presented—along with trashy serialized romance novels—quality fiction by writers like Sholem Asch, Sholem Aleichem, I. J. Singer, and I. B. Singer. I. B. Singer worked on staff throughout his adult life, and all his books were written in Yiddish (later translated) and published first in *The Forward.*

Today the Forward building, constructed in 1912 specifically to house the paper, is owned by a Chinese-American organization. Though the male and female figures centered on a sunburst above the door remain (they symbolize enlightenment), the flaming torches (socialist symbols) and portraits of Marx and Engels on the building's facade are obscured by Chinese signage. But *The Forward* is still a vital newspaper headquartered uptown. Since 1990, it has published in English as well as in Yiddish. You can buy a copy at most Manhattan newsstands.

In the heyday of the *Forverts,* the Chinese restaurant now occupying the corner of Rutgers Street and East Broadway was the Garden Cafeteria—a superb dairy restaurant where I. B. Singer and other members of the Jewish intelligentsia engaged in passionate discussions about art, literature, philosophy, and politics over blintzes and kasha varnishkes. Leon Trotsky frequently dined here when he was in New York. The Garden's walls were adorned with wonderful murals, now sadly destroyed, depicting an artisan's market that once flourished in Seward Park.

From Rutgers Street, make a left on Canal Street, bear left onto Division Street, and make a right on Eldridge Street to the:

6. **Eldridge Street Synagogue** (Congregation K'hal Adath Jeshurun), 12–16 Eldridge Street (tel. 219-0888). When it was built in 1886 by a congregation of Polish and Russian Jews, this was the most magnificent of the Lower East Side's

temples. It was also the first synagogue built by Eastern European immigrants, who had previously worshiped in converted churches. Designed by the Herter Brothers (who were also interior designers for wealthy New York families, such as the Vanderbilts), its architectural and interior decor blend Gothic, Romanesque, and Moorish styles. (Flamboyant Oriental motifs were popular in mid- to late- 19th-century synagogue architecture.) The opulent sanctuary—under a 70-foot central dome—was fitted out with an ornately carved towering walnut ark from Italy, trompe l'oeil murals, exquisite stained-glass windows, scagliola columns, and Victorian glass-shaded brass chandeliers suspended from an elaborately painted barrel-vaulted ceiling. And the grandiose terra-cotta and brick facade is highly symbolic in conception: Its cluster of five small windows represent the five books of Moses; the 12 roundels of the Gothic rose window symbolize the twelve tribes of Israel; the three points in the central pediment are for Abraham, Isaac, and Jacob; the four doors evoke Sarah, Rebeccah, Rachel, and Leah, and so on.

The congregation flourished for several decades, but as wealthy members moved away from the Lower East Side—and quota laws of the 1920s slowed new immigration to a trickle—funds became short and the building deteriorated. The immense sanctuary—which had once accommodated a congregation of 1,000 members—seemed sadly sparse when diminished to several hundred. Services moved to the basement, and the sanctuary was used only for High Holiday and wedding services. The Depression years exacerbated the synagogue's financial difficulties, and by the 1940s the main sanctuary was in such bad repair that it was boarded up. It wasn't until the 1970s that urban preservationists and historians—sparked by the interest of Gerald Wolfe, a NYU professor and architectural writer—began taking an interest in the synagogue. Wolfe formed a citizen's group to raise funds for revitalization, and his efforts led to the formation, in 1986, of the Eldridge Street Project which remains dedicated to preserving this historic edifice—today a designated landmark. The premises are currently being restored as an active synagogue and a Jewish heritage center. The temple has a small Orthodox congregation; the first bar mitzvah in more than 40 years took place here in June, 1994. There is an exhibit of old synagogue signs, mostly in Hebrew, on the premises. One reads "shul entrance for women"; another announces the coming of a famous *chazan* (cantor); a third poses and answers a question: "When is the Almighty responsive and listening to prayers? When the congregation is praying together." Note, too, the *tzedakah* (charity) box, with six slots, one for each day of the week, save the Sabbath; money in each slot is allotted for a different purpose—books, building repair, etc.

Visitors can take one-hour tours every Sunday on the hour from noon to 4pm (Monday through Thursday by appointment). Admission is charged; it goes to the very worthy cause of continuing the renovation. While you're here, inquire about the temple's many programs, lectures, and neighborhood walking tours, many of them geared to children.

Make a right on Canal Street (ahead) and a left on Essex Street, where you'll find many fascinating little shops carrying Judaica, kosher foods, and religious articles.

7. **The Bezalel Jewish Art Gallery,** 11 Essex Street (upstairs), is worth a look. Run by a Hungarian couple, Olga Geffen and Moshe Weinstock, it displays their paintings along with works by Israeli and American Jewish artists, along with antique prints and beautifully decorated *ketubahs* (Jewish marriage contracts).

Also of interest on this block is:

8. **Weinfeld's Skull Cap Mfg.,** 19 Essex Street, a century-old yarmulke factory run by succeeding generations of Weinfelds. They also make *tallith* (fringed prayer shawls worn by men during Jewish religious services, as are yarmulkes), prayer book bags, and tallith bags here.

Continue uptown toward:

9. **Essex Street Pickles** (better known as Guss Pickle Products), 35 Essex Street, which was featured in the movie *Crossing Delancey*. You'll smell the shop's briny aroma halfway down the street. An outdated sign over the awning proclaims: "Three generations of quality; please keep hands out of barrels." Guss's originated in 1910, and it's now in the fourth generation. Said barrels are filled with sours, half

sours, hot pickles, pickled tomatoes, olives, sauerkraut, horseradish, and other delicacies. Everything is made on the premises. Buy a delicious pickle to eat on the street, or purchase a jar full.

Just up the block is:

10. **Hebrew Religious Articles,** at 45 Essex Street. The shop has been here for over 50 years. Its shelves and display cases are cluttered with Jewish books, ritual phylacteries and shawls, sacred scrolls, commentaries on the Torah, menorahs, antique Judaica, electric memorial candles, seder plates, mezuzahs, yarmulkes, cantorial and Yiddish records, and a marvelous collection of turn-of-the-century Eastern European postcards.

Make a right on Grand Street to:

11. **Kossar's Bialys,** 367 Grand Street, where you can watch bakers making bialys, bagels, and *bulkas* (long bialylike rolls). Bialys were invented by bakers from the Polish town of Bialystok, and this shop has been making them since the turn of the century. Buy some oven-fresh breads to take home.

Now walk west on Grand Street and make a right into:

12. **Orchard Street.** It's hard to imagine, but Orchard Street was named for the orchards of an 18th-century farm at this location owned by James Delancey, lieutenant governor of the British province of New York (Delancey Street is named for him). In the 19th century it was a vast outdoor market-place, with rows of pushcarts lining both sides of the street. It was picturesque (though I'm sure no one thought so at the time) and vastly unsanitary.

Today pushcarts have been replaced by stores, though much of the merchandise is still displayed outside on racks. This is bargain shopping. You can save up to 50% over uptown department stores here, and many shop owners are willing to haggle over prices. However, don't expect polite service. Sundays the street is so jammed with shoppers that it is closed to vehicular traffic between Delancey and Houston Streets. But Orchard Street on Sunday is a phenomenon you must experience at least once. Come back to do serious shopping on a weekday when you have the stores to yourself.

Walk north on Orchard Street. At Broome Street, you'll come to the orientation center for the:

13. **Lower East Side Tenement Museum,** 90 Orchard Street (tel. 431-0233). Conceived as a monument to the experience of "urban pioneers" in America, this unique facility documents the lives of immigrant residents in an 1863 six-story, 22-apartment tenement. You'll be proceeding to that building (97 Orchard Street) shortly. This is where you buy tour tickets and view a 28-minute orientation video (narrated by newsman Vic Miles) called *South of Delancey.* A fascinating exhibit here is a two-sided dollhouselike model of 97 Orchard Street that shows the activities of real residents on a morning in 1870 and on a morning in 1915. All of the furnishings and settings are marvelously realistic; some of the doll's faces, created with the aid of photographs, even look like actual tenants. Be sure to pick up the information sheets that describe what is happening in each apartment tableau. Tenants are depicted preparing for Passover, doing sweatshop labor, writing letters home, dealing with illness, reading the *Forverts,* even using the chamber pot. Also on display here are Depression-era photographs of tenement life by Hungarian-born WPA artist Arnold Eagle and some of the 1,500 objects found in nooks and crannies of the building—a whisk broom, old toys, an ink bottle, an advertisement for Prof. Dora Meltzer, palmist, and others.

Over 10,000 people from 20 different countries lived here over a period of 72 years (the building was finally condemned in 1935). I daresay these immigrants would have been astonished to hear that their crowded building of cold, cramped, airless apartments—with its dim hallways and creaking floorboards—would one day be listed on the National Register of Historic Landmarks. A genealogist has collected the names of over 1,000 past tenants, which you can check for names of your own forebears.

Residents lived (and often worked, sewing "piece work" for garment manufacturers or taking in laundry) in three-room apartments with a total area of just 325 square feet! Scant light trickled through windows at distant ends of railroad flats, and the only heat came from the coal- or wood-burning stove that was also used for cooking. Large families, often supplemented by boarders for the extra cash, lived in such dwellings without running water (until the 1890s it had to be fetched from a backyard pump and hauled upstairs), indoor plumbing (until plumbing was installed at the turn of the century, chamber pots served as toilets and slops had to be carried to privies in the backyard; after that there were toilets in the hall), or electricity (which may not have been installed until the 1920s). Bed legs were often placed in kerosene, which, though it created a fire hazard, discouraged bedbugs. German immigrant owner Lucas Glockner was unhampered by building codes; few existed at the time, and even they were not enforced. By 1915, as many as 18 people sometimes occupied one apartment, sleeping in shifts. In such unhealthy conditions 40% of the babies born here died (according to 1900 census figures), and disease was rampant.

Two actual apartments, one from 1878, another from 1935 (both periods of economic depression in America), have been re-created. To further envision the lives of their occupants, keep in mind that even by 1935 the back apartments were especially dark—closely backed by other tenements, and with an elevated train roaring by at frequent intervals. Also, the indoor windows connecting rooms were not added until about 1900. The tour also visits an unrenovated apartment in the condition it was found by museum curators in the 1980s. After the tour, proceed downstairs for a slide show and to see changing art exhibits.

The museum is open Tuesday through Friday from 11am to 5pm, on Sundays from 11am to 6pm. Admission, including a tenement tour, is $7 for adults, $6 for seniors, $5 for students; children under 5 are admitted free. One-hour tours take place Monday through Friday at 1, 2, and 3pm, Sundays every 45 minutes between 11am and 5pm. Pick up a schedule of the museum's Sunday neighborhood tours for future excursions and also check out programs such as photography exhibits, slide shows, lectures, and storytelling.

Take a Break   **Ratner's Dairy Restaurant,** 138 Delancey Street, between Norfolk and Suffolk Streets (tel. 677-5588), is the oldest Jewish dairy restaurant in the city. People have been coming here since 1905 (first on Grand Street, at the present location since 1917) to feast on cheese and berry blintzes smothered in sour cream, kreplach, gefilte fish (the way Grandma used to make it), whitefish salad, potato latkes, and matzo brei. Ratner's has always been popular with New York politicos wooing the Jewish vote. Former New York Governor Nelson Rockefeller always ate here the night before elections; he said it was good luck. And during the 1989 Democratic mayoral primary, rival candidates David Dinkins and Ed Koch were surprised to run into each other at breakfast one morning; they very civilly shook hands and proceeded to devour bagels and lox. All breads and cakes are baked on the premises. A basket of scrumptious onion rolls accompanies every meal, and there are great desserts (try the strawberry cheesecake or chocolate cream pie). Open Sunday through Thursday from 6am to 11pm, Friday from 6am to 3pm, Saturday from sundown to 1am; closed Saturday mid-May through early October.

Continue uptown, past Delancey Street, to Rivington Street, where you'll make a right to reach:

14. **First Roumanian-American Congregation,** *Shaarai Shamoyim* (Gates of Heaven), at 89 Rivington Street. An Orthodox congregation bought this Romanesque Revival building, formerly a Methodist church, in 1890. Two of its esteemed cantors—Richard Tucker and Jan Peerce—went on to operatic acclaim. Today, though the synagogue still has an active congregation, the building is sadly run down. If it's open, walk up to the second floor to see the *bimàh* (altar) with brass candelabras in each corner.

Continue east to:

15. **Schapiro's Wine Company,** 126 Rivington Street. New York City's only winery, operated by three generations of the Schapiro family, has been making kosher wines for religious and secular purposes since 1899. Its founder, the present owner's grandfather, also operated a restaurant on Attorney Street, where he used to give new immigrants a free meal, a bottle of mead (honey wine), and 50¢. Free 15-minute tours are given on the hour Sundays between 11am and 4pm, but you can always sample some of the 29 varieties, which include wines made from honey, plums, blackberries, and New York State grapes, as well as French and California kosher wines. The grapes are harvested and

crushed under rabbinical supervision during the months of September and October and stored in five-thousand-gallon redwood vats on the premises. After fermentation and filtering, the wine is boiled (for religious reasons), aged in oak casks, and bottled. Only Sabbath-observant Orthodox Jews are allowed to handle the wine in preparation. Schapiro's concord and malaga are heavy and sweet in the Jewish tradition, advertised as "wine you can almost cut with a knife." Cellar walls are hung with photographs of the Lower East Side at the turn of the century. Schapiro's is open Monday through Thursday from 10am to 5pm, Fridays from 10am to 2pm, and Sundays from 11am to 4pm.

Walk back to Orchard Street and continue north, turning left on Houston Street.

Take a Break   **Katz's Delicatessen,** 205 East Houston Street, at Ludlow Street (tel. 254-2246), is a classic New York deli that's been in business at this location since 1889. The interior is little changed from those days. Even the World War II sign reading "Send a salami to your boy in the Army" is still intact. Katz's was the setting for Meg Ryan's famous faked-orgasm scene in the movie *When Harry Met Sally.*

"She didn't really fake it," says owner Fred Austin, "it was the food." During film retakes, Billy Crystal, a great Katz's fan, wolfed down the equivalent of a dozen corned beef sandwiches, which he supplemented on breaks with hot dogs, cherry peppers, and pickles! God, please give me this man's metabolism. Note the photographs in the window and lining the blond wood walls of Katz's in the old days and of famous patrons over the years—everyone from Jackie Mason to Houdini. Order up a pastrami or corned beef sandwich on rye (it's stuffed with about $^3/_4$ of a pound of meat), a potato knish, and a cream soda. Austin took over the place from the Katz family about a decade ago, but hasn't changed a thing—even the archetypical surly Jewish waiter service. "If anyone's nice to a customer, I want to hear about it," he says. There's cafeteria and waiter service. Open Sunday through Wednesday from 8am to 9pm, Thursdays from 8am to 10pm, Fridays and Saturdays from 8am to 11pm.

THE EAST VILLAGE

Start: The Strand Bookstore, at the intersection of Broadway and 12th Street.

Subway: Take the 4, 5, 6, N, or R to 14th Street/Union Square station; walk south on Broadway.

Finish: Astor Place subway kiosk.

Time: 3 to 5 hours.

Best Time: Weekdays after 9:30am, when the Strand has opened.

Worst Time: Weekends, when some places may be closed; however, even then there's plenty to see.

Like other New York City neighborhoods, the East Village has reinvented itself time and time again in the years between its inception as part of Dutch Governor Peter Stuyvesant's farm and its current incarnation as the home of the funky fringe of the city's arts and nightlife scene. From about 1840, one immigrant enclave after another filled the neighborhood's town houses and tenements, and all of these people have left their stamp here in some way—from the early Irish and German settlers to the still-extant mix of Jews (this area was the home of the Yiddish theater), African Americans, Latin Americans, Japanese, Indians, Eastern Europeans (especially Ukrainians), and Italians. Into that melting pot stir an important ingredient—latter-day-bohemian middle-class refuseniks who still arrive here daily from all over the country. This diversity is the East Village's defining characteristic.

In the 1960s and 1970s, the neighborhood was the hub of hippiedom, and, if the '60s spirit still lives anywhere, it is in the East Village. The action then centered on St. Mark's Place between Second and Third Avenues where Abbie Hoffman lived. Other major players (though we wouldn't have used that expression then) included Allen Ginsberg (he still lives here), Jerry Rubin, Timothy Leary, cartoonist R. Crumb, Paul Krassner (editor of *The Realist*), Andy Warhol, concert promoter Bill Graham, and an assortment of Indian swamis, witches and warlocks, tarot card readers, Hell's Angels, Hare Krishnas, flower children, and political radicals. East Villagers of those decades ate macrobiotic, carefully balancing yin and yang foods except for occasional yin binges on Ratner's strawberry shortcake. They lived in $30-a-month railroad flats with bathtubs in the kitchen (these same accommodations, somewhat renovated, today rent for $1,000 a month). They took yoga classes, thrilled to Janis Joplin and the Grateful Dead at the Fillmore East, danced at the Electric Circus, listened to jazz at the Five Spot, read the *East Village Other* and the *Bhagavadgita,* and took three for-a-dollar features at the St. Mark's Cinema. Psychedelic drugs were a route to nirvana and sex was safe. It was a heady, innocent, magical time.

In the 1980s the East Village took a stab at becoming the next Soho, complete with chic galleries and nightclubs, co-op conversions, and escalating rents. A declining economy towards the end of the decade seems to have rendered the nascent art scene stillborn, but trendy clubs and upscale restaurants are still thriving in the '90s. Hippies have been replaced by spike-haired punks, anarchists, and crack dealers—as well as youthful yuppie types who either can't yet afford uptown rents or simply enjoy the action of this ever-vibrant area after a heavy day on the trading floor. Old-time residents still find it jarring to see the suit-and-tie set hoisting beers at the local bars. But gentrification notwithstanding, the East Village remains one of New York's most vital districts, a last holdout of bohemianism with many fascinating sites to view and visit.

● ● ● ● ● ● ● ● ● ● ● ● ● ● ● ● ●

Begin your tour at the northeast corner of Broadway and 12th Street, where you will see a beehive of activity surrounding the:

1. **Strand Bookstore** (tel. 473-1452). This is the world's largest used bookstore and one of New York's most cherished institutions. The last survivor of Fourth Avenue's old Book Row (a lost mecca for the literary), the Strand—named for the famous London street—was founded by Benjamin Bass in 1929. Today run by his son, Fred Bass, and Fred's daughter, Nancy, it continues to be a favorite haunt of the city's rumpled intellectuals. Lee Strasberg, Anaïs Nin, and Andy Warhol were all regular customers during their lifetimes. Saul Bellow still stops by when he's in town. The store has stayed open late a few times so that Michael Jackson could peruse vintage children's books in privacy, and Sophia Loren once waited in a car outside while she sent Anna Strasberg to pick up books for her. These latter precautions notwithstanding, I can think of few places where a celebrity is less likely to be mobbed. The Strand clientele appears anything but starstruck.

"Every book," says Bass, "eventually turns up here." The store boasts "eight miles of books." At any given time its inventory comprises over $2^{1}/_{2}$ million tomes, including a huge collection of rare books on the third floor. On a recent visit I discovered a second folio Shakespeare for $50,000, a first edition of *Uncle Tom's Cabin* for $2,500, and *The Story of the Exodus* with original Marc Chagall lithographs for $35,000. You can also find signed first editions (some for as little as $15) in the rare-book section; they make great gifts. The Strand's vast variety of books (on every subject you can imagine and at low prices) includes remainders, thousands of reviewers copies (sold at half price), great art books, and hard-to-find novels. Plan a leisurely browse, both inside and at the outdoor stalls (evocative of Paris) where books are priced at 48¢ or five for $2. The Strand opens at 9:30am Monday through Saturday, at 11am on Sunday.

Walk downtown on Broadway to 11th Street. On the northwest corner is the:

2. **Cast-Iron Building.** Cast-iron architecture was the vogue
   in New York throughout the latter half of the 19th century,
   providing an economical means of embellishing buildings
   with ornate, often neoclassical facades. This one, constructed
   in 1868 to house the James McCreery Dry Goods Store, is
   one of the few buildings left standing from the stretch of
   Broadway between 23rd and 8th Streets that became known
   after the Civil War as "Ladies' Mile."

   Luxury hotels and elegant department stores such as
   McCreery's, Wanamaker's, B. Altman, and Lord and Taylor
   opened up in this area one after the other; by the 1870s and
   1880s, the high society of New York's Gilded Age enjoyed a
   splendor unrivaled in the New World. As writer Robert
   Macoy observed in 1876 (perhaps with a bit of chauvinistic
   distortion), Broadway was "the grand promenade and
   swarm[ed] with the beauty, fashion, and wealth of New York.
   No avenue or street in London or Paris or Berlin, or any of
   our cities, can be compared with it." Towards the end of
   the 19th century, New York's wealthy families moved uptown, creating fashionable neighborhoods along Park, Madison, and Fifth Avenues, and Ladies' Mile went into decline.

   When McCreery's moved uptown in 1913, the Cast-Iron
   Building was converted first to office and warehouse space,
   then in 1971 to apartments. Note its Italian Renaissance–
   style Corinthian columns and arches. The large windows
   allowed daylight to stream in during the days before electric lighting became ubiquitous. McCreery, an Irish
   immigrant who became a major New York merchandiser,
   was a patron of the arts, leaving much of his fortune to the
   Metropolitan Museum.

   Across 11th Street on the southwest corner of the intersection is the building that used to house the:

3. **St. Denis Hotel.** Opened in 1848, the St. Denis for 60
   years offered the pinnacle of luxury and fashion to visitors.
   Famous guests included everyone from Abraham Lincoln
   to eminent Parisian actress Sarah Bernhardt. In 1877,
   Alexander Graham Bell demonstrated his recently patented
   device, the telephone, to New York notables here (he called
   someone in Brooklyn). Today the building's exterior is un-
   distinguished. Much like the Cast-Iron Building—which
   was robbed of its lovely mansard roof when developers

The East Village

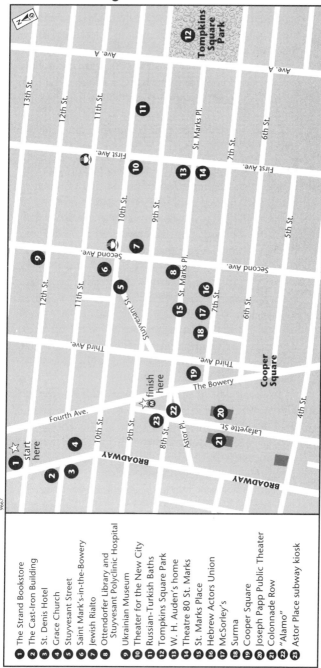

1. The Strand Bookstore
2. The Cast-Iron Building
3. St. Denis Hotel
4. Grace Church
5. Stuyvesant Street
6. Saint Mark's-in-the-Bowery
7. Jewish Rialto
8. Ottendorfer Library and Stuyvesant Polyclinic Hospital
9. Ukrainian Museum
10. Theater for the New City
11. Russian-Turkish Baths
12. Tompkins Square Park
13. W. H. Auden's home
14. Theatre 80 St. Marks
15. St. Marks Place
16. Hebrew Actors Union
17. McSorley's
18. Surma
19. Cooper Square
20. Joseph Papp Public Theater
21. Colonnade Row
22. "Alamo"
23. Astor Place subway kiosk

replaced it with a stolid two-story addition of apartments—the St. Denis suffered injury as well as insult during Broadway's decline. All of the ornamentation that once graced the exterior was removed in 1917 when the St. Denis was converted to office space. If you walk around the corner on 11th Street, you can see both of these buildings from another angle.

Continuing downtown on Broadway, immediately on your left is:

4. **Grace Church.** One of the finest examples of Gothic Revival architecture in the United States, Grace Church was built between 1843 and 1846, its adjacent rectory completed in 1847. It was the first masterpiece of famed architect James Renwick, Jr.—who would go on to design St. Patrick's Cathedral and the Smithsonian "castle" among other well-known buildings. It is humbling to almost anyone's achievements to realize that Renwick was just 23 when his plans for Grace Church were accepted! Renwick was a regular parishioner here throughout his life. A bust of him can be seen in the west corner of the north transept. The garden in front of the parish house and rectory on Broadway was created by Calvert Vaux, who designed Central Park with Frederick Law Olmsted.

In the middle of the 19th century, this was the most fashionable church in New York, with reserved pew seating costing a then-exorbitant $1,200 to $1,400. Former New York City Mayor Philip Hone wrote in his *Diary* that the stiff price of pews "may have a good effect; for many of them, though rich, know how to calculate, and if they do not go regularly to Church, they will not get the worth of their money." He described the aisles of the church as filled with "gay parties of ladies in feathers and mousseline-de-laine dresses, and dandies with moustaches and high heeled boots."

In his opening sermon at Grace Church, Dr. Thomas House Taylor exclaimed, "I do not believe that the commonest laborer who has wrought on these stones can ever look back upon his work without a feeling of reverence and awe." I know I have experienced reverence and awe viewing both the church's lovely exterior and the exquisite detail within—its beautiful carved-oak pulpit, stone carvings, magnificent windows, handsome mosaic floors, and lofty columns ascending to a vaulted ceiling. The church is constructed of hewn white marble and built in the form of a cross. Its slender marble spire—atop a 110-foot tower—dramatically marks the horizon and can be seen from as many as 20 blocks south on Broadway. Over the main entrance is a large, circular stained-glass window, and 45 additional interior Gothic windows sparkle with richly hued stained glass. Though all merit attention, note especially the five pre-Raphaelite windows by Henry Holiday along the north and south aisles of the nave depicting "Ruth and Naomi," "Joseph and Benjamin," "The Raising of Lazarus," "The Raising of Jairus' Daughter," and "The Four Marys."

The church is open for viewing from 10am to 5:45pm weekdays, Saturday noon to 4pm, Sunday during services only from 8am. For information on church programs, organ concerts, tours, and services call 254-2000.

If you follow the perimeter of the church grounds around to Fourth Avenue between 10th and 11th Streets, you can take a look at the trio of houses built decades later in a Gothic Revival style faithful to the church itself; the northern of the trio, the Grace Memorial House, was designed by Renwick himself, whereas the two others were designed by his firm. Cross the street to get a good view.

Make your way south on Fourth Avenue. At 9th Street, you'll see looming over the southwest corner of Fourth

Tom Thumb Ties the Knot

Ironically, despite its stunning architecture and traditional upper-class congregation, the most famous event ever to occur at Grace Church was a less than dignified one. P. T. Barnum arranged for the nuptials of two of his "biggest" sideshow stars, the diminutive General Tom Thumb and his like-sized bride Lavinia Warren, to be celebrated at the church. Though attended by the cream of society, their 1863 wedding exhibited all of the rowdiness and hoopla of a typical Barnum production. A parishioner who challenged sexton Isaac Hull Brown about the propriety of the affair received the response: "Even little people have the right to marry in a big church."

Avenue and Wanamaker Place the former Wanamaker Department Store Annex, another Italianate cast-iron survivor from Ladies' Mile. Centered on a skylit central court, it was a beautiful shopping venue. Today the building serves a rather unpleasant function; it's the city's Parking Violations Bureau.

Walk east on 9th Street, cross Third Avenue, and bear left onto the diagonal:

5. **Stuyvesant Street.** This street—one of the most quaint and charming in New York—is the namesake of the dour Dutch peg-legged governor of Nieuw Amsterdam, Peter Stuyvesant (1592–1672), who built a large *bouwerie* (farm) for himself on the surrounding land in the mid-1600s. Stuyvesant Street was the entrance to his property, extending all the way to the East River. The governor's descendants continued to reside in the area into the 19th century. When city officials decided in 1811 to impose the street grid that characterizes Manhattan today, the wealthy families here saved the street from being razed; it is one of the few true east-west streets in the city.

No. 21, a wide Federal-style, three-story brick building known as the Stuyvesant-Fish House, was built in 1804 for the governor's great-great-granddaughter, Elizabeth, and her husband, Nicholas Fish, a Revolutionary War hero who had served at Valley Forge. Lafayette (a close friend, as was Alexander Hamilton) visited the house on his triumphal tour in 1824. Nicholas and Elizabeth's son, Hamilton, went on to become governor of New York, a U.S. senator, and secretary of state.

Adjacent to the Stuyvesant-Fish House begins the Renwick Triangle, a group of 16 elegant brick-and-brownstone Anglo-Italianate town houses built in 1861 (nos. 23 to 35 on Stuyvesant Street and nos. 114 to 128 on 10th Street) and attributed to the aforementioned James Renwick. Architect Stanford White once lived at 118 East 10th Street. You'll have to walk around the corner to see these 10th Street houses, but before you do, note the earliest house on Stuyvesant Street, no. 44, which was built in 1795 for Nicholas William Stuyvesant, a merchant. Its splayed lintels and Flemish bond brickwork are typical of the period, and the proportions of the doorway are an indication of this residence's original grandeur. The dormer-windowed and skylit top floor is today, appropriately, an artist's studio, occupied by portrait painter Ronald Sherr, who recently painted George Bush for the National Portrait Gallery in Washington, D.C.

At the end of Stuyvesant Street, at 10th Street, is:

6. **Saint Mark's-in-the-Bowery.** This late-Georgian Episcopal stone church, completed in 1799, replaced the 1660 chapel that was part of Peter Stuyvesant's farm. To the left and right of the Italianate cast-iron portico are statues of Native Americans by Solon Borglum called "Aspiration" and "Inspiration" (Borglum's more famous brother, Gutzon, carved the heads at Mount Rushmore) and busts of Peter Stuyvesant and Daniel Tompkins. Tompkins (vice president under Monroe and a former New York governor) is buried here in the cobblestoned courtyard, along with other prominent 18th- and 19th-century New Yorkers—among them, Philip Hone (see Stop 4, above), several British colonial governors, Commodore Matthew Perry (who forced Japan to open diplomatic relations with the United States in the early 1850s), and many of Peter Stuyvesant's descendants. Actually, there is some controversy as to whether Perry is in his vault, but the vault is assuredly there. And according to some accounts, there are even graves beyond the churchyard under Second Avenue. Peter Stuyvesant's remains are embedded in the east wall of the church. St. Mark's fine Greek Revival steeple was added in 1828; its brick Parish Hall was designed by James Renwick in 1861 and its rectory by noted architect Ernest Flagg in 1900. To get a look at the interior, you have to call ahead for an appointment (tel. 674-6377) or attend a service or cultural event here. After a 1978 fire, the top stained-glass windows had to be replaced; the new windows depict life on the Lower East Side. The original bottom windows (including one depicting Peter Stuyvesant) remain intact. If the garden courtyards are open, walk in and browse around. Especially lovely is the west courtyard behind the church—a tranquil oasis with benches shaded by ancient maple and London plane trees.

For many decades, Saint Mark's has ardently supported the East Village arts community. Along with La Mama and

Caffè Cino, it was a major birthplace of off-Broadway theater, nurturing playwrights such as Sam Shepard (whose
first two plays, *Cowboys* and *Rock Garden,* were produced
here). Since 1991 Richard Foreman has been artistic director
of the Ontological Theater at St. Mark's here. Another
long-running church program is Danspace (Isadora Duncan
danced here in the 1920s, Martha Graham in the 1930s; in
more recent years the church has been used by Merce
Cunningham and other contemporary choreographers).
And the Poetry Project has featured readings by Kahlil
Gibran, William Carlos Williams, Edna St. Vincent Millay,
Carl Sandburg, Amy Lowell, Ishmael Reed, Allen Ginsberg,
W. H. Auden (a member of the parish, he sometimes used
to come to church in his bathrobe and slippers), and numerous others. Saint Mark's was also the setting for a wedding in the movie *The Group,* based on Mary McCarthy's
best seller.

Take a Break   There are numerous choices here.
Diagonally across the street from the church is the
famed **Second Avenue Deli**—a New York institution for
more than 40 years, serving up Jewish soul food nonpareil.
Everyone patronizes this deli; you might see anyone from
comic Jackie Mason to politicos like Bella Abzug or
Geraldine Ferraro at the next table. Mafia don John Gotti
was a regular before his imprisonment, even sending for
take-out during the trial. Stop in for truly authentic pastrami and corned beef piled high on fresh-baked rye,
chopped liver, kasha varnishkes, knishes, and other deli
favorites.

Other recommendables include the kitschy and
ultra-inexpensive **Ukrainian Restaurant,** 140 Second Avenue, for Eastern European specialties such as blini, pierogi,
potato pancakes, and borscht. **Telephone,** 149 Second Avenue, is a comfortable British-themed pub with a menu
listing items like shepherd's pie and fish 'n' chips in addition to quality American/continental fare. **Spaghetteria,** 178
Second Avenue, is a rather elegant but moderately priced
and trendy Italian restaurant serving first-rate pastas, sandwiches on focaccia bread, risottos, and more. At any of the
above, leave some room for a special coffee-and-dessert stop
not far ahead.

Be sure to stop in front of the Second Avenue Deli where brass stars set into the sidewalk (and the interior Molly Pecon Room) commemorate Second Avenue's heyday as the:

7. **Jewish Rialto.** New York's Jewish community increased in number and prosperity in the early years of the 20th century, and the new Jewish middle class turned Second Avenue between Houston and 14th Streets into a center of Yiddish culture. Dubbed the Yiddish Broadway, it was the site of cafés, bookstores, and a score of Yiddish-language theaters, many of them still extant through the 1950s. Actors such as Jacob Adler (father of noted drama teacher Stella Adler), and comic actors Menashe Skulnik, Boris and Bessie Thomashevsky, and Maurice Schwartz took the stage every night in plays that usually portrayed "immigrant-makes-good" themes, melodramas, and stock Yiddish comedy situations transposed to an American setting. However, Jacob Adler spearheaded a more serious dramatic movement, becoming famous for—as he always announced to his audiences—his "improved and enlarged" portrayal of King Lear and his proud version of Shylock. Thomashevsky adapted Shakespeare and Goethe to the Yiddish stage. And such well-known actors as Paul Muni, Edward G. Robinson, and Walter Matthau also came up through the Yiddish theater. It is an interesting sidenote that Jewish theater evolved in 19th-century Europe from Purim plays (holiday entertainments). Today the Yiddish Art Theatre on 12th Street and Second Avenue, which was built for Maurice Schwartz and his troupe (opening in 1926), is a multiscreen movie house. The former Café Royal across the street on the southeast corner (today a Japanese restaurant) was a celebrated haunt of Jewish intelligentsia, where habitués included Charlie Chaplin, Rachmaninoff, George Jessel, Eddie Cantor, Fannie Brice, and Moss Hart, not to mention non-Jewish Village writers such as e. e. cummings and John Dos Passos (who found it a colorful scene), and scores of aspiring poets, writers, and actors hoping to be discovered. The Royal had a sidewalk café sheltered by box hedges.

Across from the Ukrainian Restaurant, at 135–137 Second Avenue, are the:

"When I came to America and I earned three dollars a week, I spent my last cent on books or on tickets for the Yiddish theater. In those times actors were still actors and not sticks of wood. When they appeared on stage the boards burned under their feet. I saw all of them! Adler, Mme. Liptzin, Schildkraut, Kessler, Thomashevsky— every one of them. Well, and the playwrights of those times—Goldfaden, Jacob Gordin, Lateiner! Each word had to do with love, and you could have kissed each one."
—Isaac Bashevis Singer, from *Sam Palka and David Vishkover*

8. **Ottendorfer Library and Stuyvesant Polyclinic Hospital.** These two ornately embellished red-brick facilities are the 1884 gift of Anna and Oswald Ottendorfer, publishers of a German language daily newspaper called *Staats-Zeitung,* to the once-thriving Germany community of this neighborhood. Their aim was to nurture both the intellect and physical well-being of the immigrant population. Today the oldest extant branch of the New York City Public Library, the Ottendorfer's late Victorian building (with Queen Anne and Italian Renaissance influences) is adorned with terra-cotta wisdom symbols (globes, books, scrolls, owls, and torches) as well as decorative shells and fleur-de-lis. Its original name, the Freie Bibliothek und Lesehall, is still chiseled into the facade. Ottendorfer himself selected the library's original collection.

The adjacent clinic—even more elaborately adorned— features portrait busts of Hippocrates, Celsius, Galen, Humboldt, Lavoisier, and other scientists and physicians. The clinic was originally named the German Dispensary, but its administrators attempted to deflect anti-German sentiment during World War I by changing its name to the Stuyvesant Polyclinic Hospital. Both buildings were designed by architect William Schickel.

Walk north on Second Avenue past 12th Street, looking for no. 203 on your left; the fourth and fifth floors of this building house the:

9. **Ukrainian Museum** (tel. 228-0110). This small museum is committed to preserving the cultural heritage of the Ukrainian people. On permanent display—augmented by special exhibits—are an assortment of folk art items, including folk costumes and textiles displaying intricate embroideries and needlework. You can also see exquisite *pysanky* (wax-resist-decorated Easter eggs, symbols of the source of life). In ancient times these were created only by women and young girls—in secret, lest someone cast an evil spell on the egg—using fertilized eggs of chickens that had laid for the first time. The museum also displays *rushnyky* (woven and embroidered ritual cloths traditionally used as talismans in births, weddings, funerals, and calendrical rites associated with the change of seasons), ceramics, and decorative brass and silver jewelry. The collection additionally includes Ukrainian drawings, watercolors, etchings, and sculpture. You can buy examples of all the above, as well as egg-decorating kits, in the museum shop, and courses in Ukrainian folk crafts are offered. Hours are Wednesday through Sunday from 1 to 5pm. A small admission is charged.

Backtrack on Second Avenue to its intersection with 11th Street and turn left.

Take a Break Eleventh Street between First and Second Avenues is a little Little Italy, where a small Italian community still flourishes. Stop into **Veniero's Pasticceria** at no. 324—this century-old Italian bakery and café is the perfect place for cannoli and cappuccino. Veniero's is charming, with old-fashioned tile floors, beveled mirrors, an ornate pressed-copper ceiling punctuated by stained-glass skylights, and marble café tables. And its vast display cases offer myriad sweet temptations. Note, too, some marvelous Italian food shops here, such as **Russo & Son,** 344 East 11th Street, in business since 1908 and, one of my favorite New York emporia, **Ferrucci's Gourmet Market,** around the corner at 171 First Avenue. At the latter, you can pick up a loaf of fresh-baked pepperoni bread, sun-dried tomatoes, and freshly smoked mozzarella—an ambrosial sandwich combo. If you haven't eaten, Ferrucci's and Veniero's offer all you need for a fabulous picnic in Tompkins Square Park.

Walk south on First Avenue to 10th Street. Just past the southwest corner of the intersection is the:

10. **Theater for the New City.** After a quarter of a century presenting cutting-edge drama, poetry, music, dance, and the visual arts, the TNC's productions remain eclectic, politically engaged, fearless, multicultural, and creative. Go in and pick up a program or call the box office (tel. 254-1109) to find out what's on.

Cross First Avenue and walk east on 10th Street. On your right, in the middle of the block, is a venerated New York institution, the:

11. **Russian-Turkish Baths,** a.k.a. the 10th Street Baths, established in 1892. There were once numerous Turkish-style bathhouses in New York City; some of them, such as the Coney Island baths and the Luxor on 42nd Street, became the famous, or at least notorious, hangouts of gangsters and celebrities. This is the last of the genre.

Tenth Street next intersects with the first of the "Alphabet City" thoroughfares, Avenue A. Opening up from the southeast corner of the intersection is:

12. **Tompkins Square Park.** This beautiful 16-acre park (named for Daniel Tompkins; see Stop 6, above) was created on a salt marsh that was known as Stuyvesant Swamp; the Stuyvesant family gave the land to the city in 1833. It is as much a focus of the East Village as Washington Square is of Greenwich Village proper. In fact, like Washington Square, it was designed to be the hub of an upscale neighborhood—a vision that never materialized due to its out-of-the-way location. While Washington Square attracts throngs of tourists, Tompkins Square remains a true neighborhood park. Many of its surrounding buildings date to the mid-19th century.

The Slavic teenagers who staff the newsstand/soda fountain facing the park near the corner of Avenue A (no. 113) and 7th Street make great egg creams. Get yourself one, and head into the park at the 9th Street entrance. About

The 10th Street Baths

The regular patrons of the 10th Street Baths, who come here for a *schvitz* (Yiddish for sweat), are quite a heterogeneous grouping. They include Orthodox Jews, Russian wrestlers, Wall Street brokers, rap stars such as L.L. Cool J, and, on co-ed days, fashion models. John F. Kennedy, Jr., has schvitzed here, as have Frank Sinatra, Mikhail Baryshnikov, Timothy Leary, and the president of Finland. And in the early days of "Saturday Night Live," Dan Aykroyd and John Belushi used to unwind with a post-show schvitz.

The setting is far from glamorous; the dank interior of the baths evokes a 19th-century dungeon: In the Russian Room, where 11 tons of red-hot rocks raise the temperature to a scalding 195°F, patrons sit and steam, intermittently dumping buckets of ice water over their heads. Occasionally, they ask an attendant (in the old days a deaf-mute incapable of following the conversations of mobsters) for a *platza,* a vigorous scrubbing with a brush made of oak leaves (it opens the pores and lets toxins sweat away). Afterward, the bathers flop into an ice-cold pool, wrap themselves in robes, and head upstairs for sustenance and conversation over a meal of borscht, schmaltz herring, whitefish salad, kasha, and the like, as well as a few shots of vodka. The premises also house massage rooms (offering everything from shiatzu to Dead Sea salt rubs), a small gym, tanning, a redwood sauna, cots to lounge on, and a pine-fenced sundeck on the second floor amid treetops.

One man who has visited the baths several times a week for 75 years summed up his loyalty to the place: "When I walk out from here, I am like a newborn baby. . . . Why should I deny myself this little pleasure?"

Stop in for a look around and down a soul-warming shot of owner Boris Tuberman's homemade garlic and pepper vodka; for best results swallow it in one gulp and immediately stuff a cold pickled tomato into your mouth.

halfway across the 9th Street walkway into the park, through a brick portico, is an eroded monument commemorating a tragedy that was a swan song of sorts for the first immigrants to put their stamp on this area, the Germans. In 1904, the passenger ferry *General Slocum* burst into flame and sank in the East River with 1,200 aboard, most of whom were women and children from "Dutchtown" ("Dutch" being here a corruption of Deutsch) in the East Village. Many of the survivors, who lost friends and even entire families, found it emotionally impossible to continue living here after the disaster and moved to other German neighborhoods in the city. As Germans moved uptown, Eastern European Jews moved in.

Follow the park's walkways toward the southwest and, just behind the playground, you'll see the Temperance Fountain, built in 1888 in hopes of convincing the thirsty to choose water over alcoholic spirits. At the southwest corner of the park is a statue of Congressman Samuel Cox, the "Postman's Friend," whose efforts to increase salaries and improve working conditions in the U.S. Postal Service made him a sort of patron saint of letter carriers.

Over the years, Tompkins Square has frequently been the site of riots and rebellions. In the 19th and early-20th centuries, it often functioned as a venue for socialist and labor rallies. In 1874, one such gathering, resulting from a financial panic, was violently dispersed by city police, an event that became known as the Tompkins Square Massacre. Numerous peace rallies—not to mention some great rock concerts—took place here during the Vietnam War era. Occasionally, these demonstrations were broken up by the police, and hippies were routed from the park. Tensions in recent years, arising from the real estate industry's attempts to gentrify the neighborhood, have focused on the Christadora House (at the northeast corner of Ninth Street and Avenue B), which was built in 1928 as a settlement house and converted to high-priced condominiums by developers in 1987. It became the target of antigentrification forces when, in 1988, police attempted to enforce a curfew in the park and an ugly riot ensued. Officers clubbed and arrested not only protesters but innocent bystanders, and vandals did extensive damage to the Christadora. In the

1990s, the park has been extensively renovated and an encampment of homeless people were forced to move elsewhere.

These tumultuous events notwithstanding, the park is essentially a recreational setting: Children cavort in playgrounds, there's lively action on the basketball courts, swimmers cool off in the pool (open every summer), and people sunbathe on expanses of lawn and picnic under ancient elms.

Leave the park on the Avenue A side and stroll west along St. Marks Place, which is lined with casual neighborhood cafés. Just across First Avenue on the north side of the street is:

13. **W. H. Auden's home,** at 77 St. Marks Place. Auden lived and worked in a third floor apartment here (amid a clutter of books and manuscripts) from 1953 to 1972—a year before his death. Although he generally kept a low profile in the neighborhood, he was a parishioner at St. Mark's-in-the-Bowery (see Stop 6, above) and occasionally breakfasted on scotch or otherwise patronized the still-extant Holiday Cocktail Lounge next door (no. 75). Earlier in the century, the Russian Communist periodical *Novy Mir* was published at no. 77. Leon Trotsky, a contributor, came by when he visited New York in 1917.

Across the street is:

14. **Theatre 80 St. Marks.** Until the advent of VCRs, revival cinema houses flourished in New York. This 160-seat facility was one of the last, and most cherished, of the genre. It opened originally as a live theater in 1967; its first show, *You're a Good Man Charlie Brown,* played to sellout audiences for 4^1/$_2$ years. From 1971 on, proprietor Howard Otway, a former stage actor, dreamt up appealing double features and made his theater a shrine to the silver screen, adorned with photographs of the matinee idols of yesteryear. But after Otway died in 1993, his son, Lawrence Otway, decided to use the space for theatrical productions once more. The last of the classic double features, *High Moon* and *Shane,* played June 31, 1994. Today, 80 St. Marks is the home of a classical repertory group called the Pearl Theatre Company, which for 10 years was located in Chelsea. Its opening season included productions of *King Lear,*

Oedipus at Colonus by Sophocles, *The Beaux Strategem* (a Restoration comedy by George Farquhar), Carlo Goldoni's *The Venetian Twins* (a rambunctious 1748 Italian commedia dell'arte), and George Bernard Shaw's *Mrs. Warren's Profession.* Unlike so many contemporary theater companies, the Pearl does traditional interpretations of classic plays. Call the box office at 596-9802 to find out about current productions.

Follow this street west and you will soon reach the surreal center of the East Village counterculture:

15. **St. Marks Place,** between Second and Third Avenues. Today populated by punks, anarchists, and various street people who defy categorization, this hippie mecca of the 1960s and 1970s has declined to a state of general seediness. Adding insult to injury, it is besmirched by a branch of the Gap, as astonishing an advent in the East Village as the appearance of McDonald's on the Champs-Elysées. One landmark of days gone by is the Gem Spa, at the corner of Second Avenue, ever and always the area's most famous egg cream venue. On the north side of the block, the bright blue building occupying nos. 19–25 was once home to the Electric Circus, the disco that succeeded Andy Warhol's Exploding Plastic Inevitable (a multimedia event combining his films with live music, dancing, light show effects, and bizarre live action) at a bar called the Dom below. In these more somber times, the building houses the All-Craft Foundation, an organization that helps homeless and drug-addicted people in the community. Funky shops along the street sell cheap jewelry, Kurt Cobain T-shirts, leather, and tapes and CDs, augmented—unless there has recently been a bust—by peddlers hawking used books and incense.

Make your way back to Second Avenue and turn right, then turn right again onto 7th Street. On the north side of the street, at no. 31, look for the granite facade into which is carved the name of the:

16. **Hebrew Actors Union.** During the heyday of Yiddish theater on Second Avenue, even the biggest stars used to pay regular visits to this building. Today, despite the almost total demise of the Jewish Rialto, the union is still active.

Further along is one of the few vestiges of the days when the East Village had a significant Irish population:

17. **McSorley's Old Ale House and Grill,** 15 East 7th Street (tel. 473-9148), New York's oldest watering hole, established in 1854. It looks—and smells—every bit its age, an effect enhanced by the old potbellied stove that radiates heat in winter months. The wood floor is strewn with sawdust, and the pressed-tin walls are cluttered with a thicket of photos and newspaper clippings—all gone yellow with age and a century's worth of tobacco smoke—interspersed with an odd assortment of knick-knacks and mementos. Over the years, luminaries from Peter Cooper to Brendan Behan have earned the right to a particular chair or bar stool, and the bar's beery charm was captured in Joseph Mitchell's *New Yorker* stories, later collected in a book, *McSorley's Wonderful Saloon.* Artist John Sloan also immortalized the saloon's unique atmosphere in a painting called "A Mug of Ale at McSorley's" (1913). Perhaps the only significant change McSorley's has undergone in this century occurred in 1971, when a group of women successfully challenged its men-only policy. If you drop in on an afternoon for a mug of ale (the food here, deli sandwiches and chili, is not notable), you might just catch a glimpse of the New York that Peter Cooper knew.

McSorley's is really an anachronism on 7th Street these days, which is now the heart of a Ukrainian immigrant community some 20,000 strong. Representative of this is:

18. **Surma,** a store–cum–community center at no. 11, selling Ukrainian newspapers and books and Eastern European handicrafts. The latter include embroidered peasant blouses (Karen Allen wore one in the film *Raiders of the Lost Ark),* paintings, traditional porcelain, dolls, and *pysanky* (decorated eggs). According to legend, *pysanky* conquer evil, and only if enough eggs are painted will the forces of good triumph. So buy an egg-decorating kit and get busy. Across the street, note St. George's Ukrainian Catholic Church, its dome adorned with 16 beautiful stained-glass windows.

Across Third Avenue from 7th Street is:

19. **Cooper Square.** Situated on this wedge-shaped lot are the chocolate-brown Cooper Union Foundation Building and a small park housing a bronze likeness of Peter Cooper (1791–1883)—inventor, industrialist, philanthropist, and one of the great geniuses of his day. He made the bulk of his fortune through an ironworks and a glue factory, built the first steam locomotive in the United States (the *Tom Thumb*), developed the first rolled-steel railroad rails, and was instrumental in laying the first transatlantic telegraph cable. Cooper, a self-educated man from modest roots, believed that his wealth carried with it a responsibility to improve the working man's situation, and so he founded the Cooper Union to provide free education in the practical trades and arts to any man or woman who wished to attend. A sense of Cooper as a benevolent, fatherly figure flows from the statue, and it's only natural: The sculptor, Augustus Saint-Gaudens, was able to attend Cooper Union's art school because of its founder's characteristic generosity.

Enter the Cooper Union Foundation Building and go to the rear of the lobby to see an elaborate and amusing carved-wood birthday card given to the founder by the senior class of 1871, thanking him for his 80th-birthday gift of $150,000 to the school. A staircase in the lobby leads down to the Great Hall; in keeping with Peter Cooper's designs for it, the Great Hall has functioned over the years as a free public forum in which great issues of the day are debated. Labor leader Samuel Gompers, free-love advocate Victoria Woodhull, and Sioux chief Red Cloud all spoke here, but perhaps the Great Hall's most famous moment occurred in 1860, when Abraham Lincoln's fiery "right makes might" antislavery speech carried public opinion in New York and sped him to the Republican Party's presidential nomination.

Walk around Cooper Union, turn left on Astor Place, then hang another left onto Lafayette Street, which in the 1850s was the city's most elegant residential boulevard. A few paces down on your left is the:

20. **Joseph Papp Public Theater.** The Public, one of New York's most vital cultural institutions, is housed in the old Astor Library. This red-brick palazzo, the first public library in New York City, was the lone public bequest of John Jacob

Astor, who made millions in the fur trade and was a notoriously tightfisted landowner. In 1911 the library's collection was moved to the New York Public Library on 42nd Street. From 1920 to 1966, the Hebrew Immigrant Aid Society used the building to shelter and feed thousands of Jewish immigrants and help them gain a footing in the United States. When they moved elsewhere, city officials and Joseph Papp's New York Shakespeare Festival rescued the Astor Library from a developer who had planned to raze it to make way for an apartment complex; the building was designated a city landmark and became the permanent indoor home of the New York Shakespeare Festival.

The Public Theater opened in 1967 with the original production of *Hair,* which moved on to Broadway; in 1975 *A Chorus Line* followed suit, becoming the longest-running show in Broadway history. Over the years, the New York Shakespeare Festival has presented on the Public's five stages new plays by such major playwrights as David Rabe, John Guare, David Mamet, Caryl Churchill, Sam Shepard, and Larry Kramer. Founder Joseph Papp died in 1992, but the theater continues to thrive, with cinema offerings, poetry readings, lectures, a café, a bookstore, and a late-night cabaret added to its offerings. A show here makes for a wonderful evening; unsold tickets are often available as half-price "Quiktix" after 6pm (1pm for matinees on Saturday and Sunday) in the lobby.

Across the street from the Public Theater is:

21. **Colonnade Row,** a group of row houses fronted by a crumbling marble colonnade. They were originally christened La Grange Terrace after the Marquis de Lafayette's country estate, just outside Paris. Of the nine row houses built by developer Seth Geer in 1831, only four remain; the five on the south end were demolished to make room for the Wanamaker Department Store warehouse. When built, these houses were fronted by 30-foot gardens and Lafayette Street was a quiet, posh residential district; John Jacob Astor lived here, as did members of the Vanderbilt and Delano families and writer Washington Irving. President John Tyler married Franklin Delano's daughter, Julia, here in 1844. The fashionable set moved uptown after the Civil War and these houses have been in decline ever since, but if you look

at the roof of no. 434 (the Astor Place Theater is on the ground floor), you'll see the carved-stone honeysuckle-leaf border that once stretched across all nine houses.

Turn back and walk toward Astor Place. The black metal sculpture that dominates the traffic island in the middle of the intersection is the:

22. **"Alamo,"** known universally to area residents as "the Cube." Sculptor Tony Rosenthal built the piece in 1967 for a city-sponsored exhibition. He is reportedly pleased that the "Alamo" has become a participatory piece—it was built on a rotating post so that it could be positioned after installation, but it has become a tradition in the East Village for anyone feeling a bit rowdy to spin the Cube.

The next and last stop is on the adjoining traffic island across 8th Street, the:

23. **Astor Place subway kiosk.** Earlier in this century, almost every IRT subway stop in Manhattan had a kiosk much like this one. The Transit Authority inexplicably decided to tear them all down in 1911, but when the Astor Place subway station was restored in 1985, officials revived what had been a lost element of New York City's architectural scene. (Down in the station, Milton Glaser's mosaics and the ceramic low-relief tiles depicting beavers—the animal whose pelt made John Jacob Astor's fortune—are worth a look.) Peter Cooper would no doubt have been deeply satisfied to know that the architect of the new kiosk was a Cooper Union graduate.

GREENWICH VILLAGE LITERARY TOUR PART I

Start: St. Luke's Place and Hudson Street.

Subway: Take the 1 or 9 to Houston Street and walk northwest to the starting point.

Finish: The White Horse Tavern at Hudson and 11th Streets.

Time: Approximately 3 to 4 hours, not including lunch.

Best Time: Any time the weather is conducive to walking.

As a teenager growing up in New York in the early 1960s I was wildly drawn to the mystique of Greenwich Village. There, I believed, life was lived with a passionate intensity, verve, and dark drama that were largely absent from my prosaic middle-class home. And my forays into its mysterious winding streets—where a jewelry store had a snake for a door handle and where ethnically diverse groups gathered over folk music in Washington Square Park—confirmed my most rosily decadent expectations. In those days, alienated beatnik bongo drummers pounded out primitive rhythms in dimly lit, smoke-filled nightclubs, and the wildly experimental Living Theater invited audience members to mingle with druggy jazz musicians onstage.

The Village has always attracted rebels, radicals, and creative types—from earnest 18th-century revolutionary Tom Paine, to early-20th-century radicals such as John Reed and Mabel Dodge, to the Stonewall rioters who gave birth to the gay liberation movement by resisting a routine police bust in 1969. It was even a Village protest in 1817 that saved the area's colorfully convoluted lanes and byways when the city imposed a geometric grid system on New York streets.

Almost every American writer you can think of has, at some time, made his or her home in the Village. As early as the 19th century it was already New York's literary hub—venue for salons and other gatherings of the intelligentsia. And both the Metropolitan Museum of Art and the Whitney Museum of American Art came into being on 8th Street, albeit some 60 years apart. The 20th century saw this area transformed from an aristocratic neighborhood and bastion of old New York families to a bohemian enclave of struggling writers and artists. Though skyrocketing rents made the Village less accessible to starving artists after the late 1920s, it remained a mecca for creative people—so much so that almost every building is a literary landmark.

Though the focus of this tour—and the following one—is the Village's literary history, I think you'll also enjoy strolling its quaint, tree-lined streets; between stops, be sure to notice the beautiful Federal and Greek Revival buildings along our route.

● ● ● ● ● ● ● ● ● ● ● ● ● ● ● ● ●

Starting Out **Anglers & Writers,** 420 Hudson Street (tel. 675-0810), is a delightful place to enjoy breakfast before you begin the tour. Its very pretty interior features flower-bedecked tables, antique oak furnishings, and walls hung with wicker baskets and copper pots. Breakfast/brunch options include fresh-baked scones and fruit breads, pancakes swimming in brandied maple syrup, and cinnamon sour-cream coffee cake—along with a wide selection of teas and coffees. Homemade desserts are irresistible. It opens at 9am Monday through Saturday, 10am on Sunday.

1. **6 St. Luke's Place.** St. Luke's Place is lined with stately gingko trees and elegant mid-19th-century Italianate houses.

Several well-known writers have occupied its impressive dwellings. This particular brick town house, however, is not a literary landmark. It was the residence of the flamboyant Jimmy Walker when he was mayor of New York, though he was seldom on the premises (he preferred to sleep at the Ritz-Carlton or the Mayfair). Actually, Walker did write something—a 1908 hit song called "Will You Love Me in December as You Do in May?" Later, Governor Alfred E. Smith quipped of the charming but thoroughly unreliable mayor, "If you make a date with Jim in December, he will keep it next May." Walker was notorious for frequenting speakeasies even during the height of Prohibition, and for enjoying an extravagant lifestyle while the Tammany Hall bosses tightened their grip on the city. But New Yorkers adored him, and Walker loved New York (even though he spent nearly a quarter of his first two years in office—1925 to 1927—on out-of-town pleasure trips). When scandal forced him to resign as mayor, Walker sailed for Europe with his wife (a former showgirl). The park across the street, which was built over an 18th-century cemetery, is named for him; it is said that walking around this cemetery inspired the gloomy Edgar Allan Poe's 1838 novel *The Narrative of Arthur Gordon Pym.*

As you continue, you'll pass no. 10, which you may recognize from exterior shots of the Huxtable home in *The Cosby Show.*

Our next stop is:

2. **12 St. Luke's Place.** Sherwood Anderson, hailed as the authentic voice of the Midwest after publishing *Winesburg, Ohio* in 1919, lived in a basement apartment here in 1923 following what he described as a year of "devastating intensity of feeling." (In 1922 his second marriage—one of four, to the free-spirited Tennessee Mitchell—had come to an end.) Midwest voice notwithstanding, Anderson once said: "When an American stays away from New York too long, something happens to him. Perhaps he becomes a little provincial, a little dead, a little afraid."

At St. Luke's Place, Anderson was thrilled to learn that fellow midwesterner Theodore Dreiser, whom he idolized, lived three doors down. In 1916, he had written a tribute to Dreiser that had been published in the *Little Review:*

> *To Theodore Dreiser*
> *In whose presence I have sometimes had*
> *the same refreshed feeling as when in*
> *the presence of a thoroughbred horse.*

Steeling himself to meet his mentor, Anderson knocked timidly on Dreiser's door and announced himself, only to have the painfully shy and sensitive Dreiser slam the door in his face. Later that afternoon, Dreiser sent a note of apology and invited Anderson to a party he was giving. It was the inauspicious beginning of a lifelong friendship.

Further along the block is:

3. **14 St. Luke's Place,** where poet Marianne Moore shared a ground-floor apartment with her mother from 1918 to 1929. Their rent was $25 a month. Alfred Kreymborg, to whose many literary magazines Moore contributed, described her as "an astonishing person with Titian hair, a brilliant complexion and a mellifluous flow of polysyllables which held every man in awe."

First published during World War I, she was much praised in Europe by expatriates T. S. Eliot and Ezra Pound. Her poems abound with vivid images of nature—the "phosphorescent alligator," "a scared frog, screaming like a bird," "crow-blue mussel shells," and "porcupine-quilled palm trees that rattle like the rain."

While living at 14 St. Luke's, Moore wrote to Pound: "Henry James, Blake, the minor prophets and Hardy, are so far as I know, the direct influences bearing on my work." In the same letter she spoke of her residence: "I like New York, the little quiet part of it in which my mother and I live. I like to see the tops of the masts from our door and to go to the wharf and look at the craft on the river."

Continue to:

4. **16 St. Luke's Place.** Theodore Dreiser lived on the parlor floor of this classic New York brownstone from 1922 to 1923 and wrote much of *An American Tragedy* here. He is unflatteringly described in the *Cambridge Biographical Dictionary* as "a large, egocentric man with an excessive sexual appetite" whose "reputation was sullied by his jealousy of Sinclair Lewis's receipt of the Nobel prize for literature in

Greenwich Village Literary Tour Part I

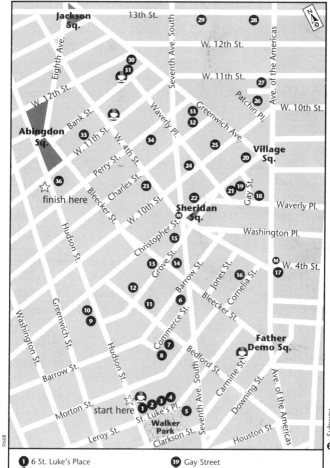

1 6 St. Luke's Place
2 12 St. Luke's Place
3 14 St. Luke's Place
4 16 St. Luke's Place
5 Hudson Park Library
6 11 Commerce St.
7 75 1/2 Bedford St.
8 Cherry Lane Theatre
9 St. Luke in the Fields
10 487 Hudson St.
11 Chumley's
12 17 Grove St.
13 45 Grove St.
14 309 Bleecker St.
15 59 Grove St.
16 33 Cornelia St.
17 Sixth Avenue and West 4th Street
18 139 Waverly Place

19 Gay Street
20 11 Christopher St.
21 Waverly Place and Christopher Street
22 The Lion's Head
23 238 West 4th St.
24 165 West 10th St.
25 139 West 10th St.
26 Patchin Place
27 118 West 11th St.
28 138 West 13th St.
29 152 West 13th St.
30 91 Greenwich Ave.
31 5 Bank St.
32 15 Charles St.
33 45 Greenwich Ave.
34 38 Perry St.
35 263 West 11th St.
36 The White Horse Tavern

1930 and by his alleged plagiarism of a book on Russia by Dorothy Thompson, Lewis's wife." Son of an impoverished German immigrant, Dreiser left his Terre Haute, Indiana, home at the age of 15 to become a journalist. He was 29 when his first book, the controversial *Sister Carrie,* was published in 1900. He once told H. L. Mencken he had planned his last words. They were "Shakespeare, I come!" I don't know if he managed to utter them.

Across the street is:

5. **The Hudson Park Library,** which has served the Village community since 1906. Poet Marianne Moore worked here as an assistant librarian from 1921 to 1925, earning $50 a month. The head librarian there originally asked Moore's mother if she thought Marianne, a voracious reader, would like to work at the library. Her mother said she thought not, since, as the shoemaker's children never have shoes, Marianne would probably feel, if she joined the library staff, she would no longer have time to read. However, when informed of the offer, Moore was immediately enthusiastic and enjoyed her work there very much.

Take a Break You can enjoy an excellent leisurely lunch at **Cent' Anni,** 50 Carmine Street, between Bedford and Bleecker Streets (tel. 989-9494). Be sure to order the scrumptious *zuppa ortolana*—a baked soup rich with beans, cabbage, and leeks, topped with toast and fresh-grated parmesan—a meal in itself. Lunch entrées average about $16, but you can get by for less with pastas and antipasti. Cent' Anni is an attractive restaurant, with bleached oak floors and white-linened tables; walls are hung with photographs and oil paintings of Italy. Open for lunch Monday through Friday from noon to 3pm.

From St. Luke's Place, make a left on Seventh Avenue and head uptown. Then turn left on Commerce Street to reach:

6. **11 Commerce Street.** Washington Irving wrote *The Legend of Sleepy Hollow* while living in this quaint three-story brick building. Born into a prosperous New York family, he was sent for a long sojourn in Europe (for health reasons) in his early 20s. As an officer in the War of 1812 he penned biographies of naval heroes. In 1819, under the name

Geoffrey Crayon, he wrote *The Sketch Book,* which contained the stories of *The Legend of Sleepy Hollow, Westminster Abbey,* and *Rip Van Winkle.* Irving was one of the elite New Yorkers who served on the planning commission for Central Park, and, from 1842 to 1846, he was the American ambassador to Spain. He coined the phrase "the almighty dollar," and once observed that "A tart temper never mellows with age, and a sharp tongue is the only tool that grows keener with constant use."

Continue walking west on Commerce and turn left at Bedford Street to find:

7. **75½ Bedford Street.** The narrowest house in the Village (a mere 9½ feet across), this unlikely three-story brick residence was built on the site of a former carriage alley in 1873. Pretty red-headed feminist poet Edna St. Vincent Millay, who arrived in the Village fresh from Vassar, lived here from 1923 (the year she won a Pulitzer Prize for her poetry) to 1925. Ever a favorite among Village intelligentsia, the vivacious Millay perhaps best expressed her youthful passion for life in the lines:

> *My candle burns at both ends;*
> *It will not last the night;*
> *But ah, my foes, and oh, my friends—*
> *It gives a lovely light!*

Though Millay left the Village at age 33, moving with her Dutch husband, Eugen Boissevain, to a 700-acre farm in upstate New York, she left her mark and is remembered as a quintessential Village bohemian. Other famous occupants of the narrow house include Cary Grant and John Barrymore. The house, which is in a considerable state of disrepair, has seen better days. What seems the front door, by the way, is really the back; the front entrance is in a courtyard behind the building.

Return to Commerce Street, and turn left, where:

8. **The Cherry Lane Theatre,** nestled in a bend at 38 Commerce Street, was founded in 1924 by Edna St. Vincent Millay. Famed scenic designer Cleon Throckmorton transformed the Revolutionary-era building (originally a silo on a farm here, later a brewery and a box factory) into a playhouse that

presented works by Edward Albee, Samuel Beckett (*Waiting for Godot* and *Endgame* premiered here), Eugene Ionesco, Jean Genet, and Harold Pinter. In 1951, Judith Malina and Julian Beck founded the ultra-experimental Living Theatre on its premises. And before rising to megafame, Barbra Streisand worked as a Cherry Lane usher.

At the end of Commerce Street, make a left onto Barrow Street and a right on Hudson Street. On the west side of Hudson, at Grove Street, is:

9. **St. Luke in the Fields,** one of the oldest churches in Manhattan, built in 1822. At that time it was a country church, surrounded by farmland; visiting city folk arrived by riverboat or stagecoach. The original chapel was gutted by fire in 1981, but neighborhood residents came to the rescue with contributions to finance its rebuilding. One of St. Luke's founding vestrymen was Clement Moore, who, while most famous for his holiday poem, *A Visit From St. Nicholas* (better known as *'Twas the Night Before Christmas*), was also a serious scholar who compiled Hebrew and Greek lexicons. St. Luke was the venue for Dylan Thomas's funeral.

Next door is:

10. **487 Hudson Street.** This 1827 house, presently the Parish House of St. Luke, was a boyhood home of Bret Harte, author of *The Luck of Roaring Camp* and other colorfully evocative stories inspired by a trip to California with his mother, when he was 15, during the height of the Gold Rush. About these works Harte said, "I cannot claim . . . any higher motive than to illustrate an era of which Californian history has preserved the incidents more often than the character of the actors . . . an era replete with a certain heroic Greek poetry, of which perhaps none were more unconscious than the heroes themselves." Harte wrote some of his most famous poems (among them, *John Burns of Gettysburg* and *The Society upon the Stanislau)* when he was secretary of the U.S. Mint in San Francisco from 1864 to 1870. During his lifetime, he published 44 volumes of poetry and prose.

Now turn right onto Grove Street and make another right on Bedford Street to:

11. **Chumley's,** 86 Bedford Street (tel. 675-4449), opened in 1926 in a former blacksmith's shop. During Prohibition it was a speakeasy with a casino upstairs. Its convoluted entranceway with four steps up and four down (designed to slow police raiders), the lack of a sign outside, and a back door that opens on an alleyway to Barrow Street are remnants of that era. Original owner Lee Chumley was a radical labor sympathizer who held secret meetings of the IWW on the premises. Chumley's has long been a writer's bar. Walls are lined with book jackets of works by famous patrons who, over the years, have included Edna St. Vincent Millay (she once lived upstairs), John Steinbeck, Eugene O' Neill, e. e. cummings, Edna Ferber, John Dos Passos, F. Scott Fitzgerald, Theodore Dreiser, William Faulkner, Gregory Corso, Norman Mailer, William Carlos Williams, Allen Ginsberg, Lionel Trilling, Harvey Fierstein, Calvin Trillin, and numerous others. Even the elusive J. D. Salinger hoisted a few at the bar here, and Simone de Beauvoir came by when she was in town. With its working fireplaces (converted blacksmith forges), wood-plank flooring, old carved-up oak tables, and amber lighting, Chumley's lacks nothing in the way of mellowed atmosphere. Think about returning for drinks or dinner. A blackboard menu features fresh pasta and grilled fish. Open nightly from 5pm to an arbitrary closing time, Chumley's also offers brunch on weekends from 11am to 4pm.

Double back to Grove Street, which was named in the 19th century for its many gardens and groves, and make a right to:

12. **17 Grove Street.** Parts of this picturesque wood-frame house date to the early 1800s. Originally, it was the home of William Hyde, a window-sash maker. The top floor was added in 1870, and the present owners created a downstairs level in 1989. A friend of James Baldwin's lived here in the 1960s, and Baldwin frequently stayed at the house. Baldwin, whose fiery writings coincided with the inception of the civil rights movement, once said, "The most dangerous creation of any society is that man who has nothing to lose."

Further along is:

13. **45 Grove Street.** Originally a freestanding two-story building, this was, in the 19th century, one of the Village's most elegant mansions, surrounded by verdant lawns with greenhouses and stables on the premises. Built in 1830, it was refurbished with Italianate influences in 1870. In the movie *Reds,* based on the life of John Reed, 45 Grove was portrayed as Eugene O'Neill's house, though O'Neill never lived here.

   Ohio-born poet Hart Crane (see also Walking Tour 6, Stop 30) rented a second-floor room at 45 Grove in 1923, and began writing his poetic portrait of America, *The Bridge* (Hart depicted the Brooklyn Bridge as a symbol of America's westward expansion). Frustrated by frequent rejection from magazines and other exigencies of his craft, Crane would occasionally toss his typewriter out the window. Often moody and despondent, he was chronically in debt, plagued by guilt over homosexual encounters on the nearby docks, and given to almost nightly alcoholic binges; fellow Villager e. e. cummings once found him passed out on a sidewalk, bundled him into a taxi, and had him driven home. In 1932, returning by ship from Mexico (where, on a Guggenheim fellowship, he had been attempting to write an epic poem about Montezuma), Crane committed suicide at the age of 33 by leaping overboard into the Atlantic. His works became famous only after his death.

   Continue on Grove Street, make a right at Bleecker Street, and look for:

14. **309 Bleecker Street.** Thomas Paine lived in a small two-story wooden house at this location, today a Gristede's supermarket. Originally Barrow Street, a half block away, was named Reason Street (for *The Age of Reason*) in Paine's honor. Later the name was corrupted to Raisin Street and eventually it was changed to Barrow.

   Head east on Bleecker Street, turn left on Seventh Avenue, and walk uptown for a block. To your left is:

15. **59 Grove Street.** English-born American revolutionary/political theorist/writer Thomas Paine died here in 1809. Paine came to America (with the help of Benjamin Franklin) in 1774, and in 1776 produced his famous pamphlet, *The Crisis,* which begins with the words: "These are the times

that try men's souls. The summer soldier and the sunshine patriot will, in this crisis, shrink from the service of their country." After fighting in the American Revolution, he returned to England to advocate the overthrow of the British monarchy. Indicted for treason, he escaped to Paris, becoming a French citizen; while imprisoned there during the Terror, he wrote *The Age of Reason.* He returned to the U.S. in 1802, where he was vilified for his atheism. Benjamin Franklin once said to Paine, "Where liberty is, there is my country." To which Paine replied: "Where liberty is not, there is mine."

The downstairs space has always been a restaurant, today **Marie's Crisis Cafe** (tel. 243-9323). Though the building Paine lived in burned down, some of the interior brickwork is original. Of note, behind the bar, is a WPA-era mural (done with metals on mirror) depicting the French and American Revolutions and bearing the mottoes *"Liberté, Egalité, Fraternité"* and "Rights of Man." Up a flight of stairs is another mural (a wood-relief carving) called *La Convention.* It depicts Robespierre, Danton, and Thomas Paine, and is inscribed with Danton's inspirational words of 1792, "De l'audace, et encore de l'audace, et toujours de l'audace!" In the 1920s, you might have spotted anyone from Eugene O'Neill to Edward VIII of England here. Today, Marie's is a lively piano bar (everyone sings along nightly from 9:30pm to 3:30am).

Return to Seventh Avenue and double back downtown again. Turn left on Bleecker Street, then left on Cornelia, and look for:

16. **33 Cornelia Street.** Throughout the 1940s, film critic/poet/novelist/screenwriter James Agee lived on Bleecker Street and worked in a studio at this address. Here he completed final revisions on the text of *Let Us Now Praise Famous Men,* which, along with Walker Evans' evocative photographs, portrayed the bleak lives of Alabama sharecroppers. The book originated in 1936 as an article for Henry Luce's *Fortune* magazine, which rejected the piece as too long and too liberal. This isn't surprising, since the book's first pages contain a paraphrase from Marx's *Communist Manifesto:* "Workers of the world, unite and fight. You have nothing to lose but your chains, and a world to win."

Though a Harvard grad from an upper-class background, Agee was extremely sympathetic to the plight of the poor (he once took a hobo into his home); dubious—if not downright cynical—about the very nature of journalism; and ashamed of the intrusive nature of his mission. "It seems to me . . . ," he wrote, "obscene and thoroughly terrifying . . . to pry intimately into the lives of an undefended and appallingly damaged group of human beings, an ignorant and helpless rural family, for the purpose of parading the nakedness, disadvantage, and humiliation of these lives before another group of human beings, in the name of . . . honest journalism . . . of humanity, of social fearlessness, for money, and for a reputation for crusading . . ."

Agee later worked as a movie reviewer for both *Time* and the *Nation*—sometimes concurrently, reviewing the same films differently for each magazine. He also wrote the movie script for *The African Queen.* The building is fronted by what was an early 1800s blacksmith shop.

Nearby, at 31 Cornelia Street, once stood the **Caffè Cino,** which opened as a coffeehouse in 1958, serving cappuccino in shaving mugs. In the early 1960s, owner Joe Cino began to encourage aspiring playwrights—such as Lanford Wilson, Sam Shepard, and John Guare—to stage readings and performances in his cramped converted storefront space. Experimentation in this tiny café space gave birth to New York's off-off-Broadway theater. Plagued by money troubles, Cino committed suicide in 1967; Caffè Cino closed a year later.

At the end of Cornelia Street you'll come to the junction of:

17. **Sixth Avenue and West 4th Street.** Eugene O'Neill, a heavy drinker, nightly frequented a bar called the Golden Swan (more familiarly known as the "Hell Hole" or "Bucket of Blood") at this corner and later used it as a setting for his play *The Iceman Cometh*—a play that was 12 years in the writing. The bar was patronized by prostitutes, gangsters (most notably an Irish gang called the Hudson Dusters), longshoremen, anarchists, and politicians, as well as artists (John Sloan did a painting of it) and writers. Eccentric owner Tom Wallace (on whom O'Neill modeled saloon proprietor Harry Hope) kept a pig in the basement

and seldom ventured off the premises. A recycling center occupies the bar's former site.

Head north on Sixth Avenue for a couple of blocks and make a left on Waverly Place to reach:

18. **139 Waverly Place.** Edna St. Vincent Millay lived here with her sister, Norma, in 1918. Radical playwright Floyd Dell, her lover, who found the apartment for her, commented: "She lived in that gay poverty which is traditional of the Village, and one may find vivid reminiscences of that life in her poetry." An interesting note: Edna St. Vincent Millay's middle name was derived from St. Vincent's Hospital, which had saved the life of her uncle.

Continue walking west, and make a right at:

19. **Gay Street.** Famous residents of this tiny street (originally a stable alley) have included New York Mayor Jimmy Walker, who owned the 18th-century town house at no. 12. A more recent owner of the building was Frank Paris, creator of *Howdy Doody.*

In the 1920s, Ruth McKenney lived in the basement of no. 14 with her sister Eileen, who later married Nathanael West. It was the setting for McKenney's zany *My Sister Eileen* stories, which were first published in the *New Yorker,* then collected into a book. They were then turned into a popular stage comedy that ran on Broadway from 1940 to 1942, followed by a Broadway musical version called *Wonderful Town* and two movie versions, one of them starring Rosalind Russell as Ruth. The house dates to 1827.

Mary McCarthy, the *Partisan Review's* drama critic and author of *The Group,* lived in a studio apartment at no. 18 in the 1940s. During Prohibition there were several speakeasies on the street.

On the other side of Gay Street is:

20. **11 Christopher Street.** In 1918, e. e. cummings and William Slater Brown shared an apartment at this address, today a parking lot. Cummings and Brown (a pal from Harvard days) had both been imprisoned for several months while stationed in France as ambulance drivers during World War I. The charge: writing letters that military censors regarded (erroneously) as treasonous. Basically, the two young men (Brown was 21, Cummings 23) seemed to view the

whole experience as a lark. Cummings wrote home to his parents, "Our life here is A 1. Never have I so appreciated leisure. I continually write notes on painting, poetry, and sculpture, as well as music, and the Muse Herself has not been unkind." Another letter describes "days spent with an inimitable friend [Brown] in soul-stretching probings of aesthetics . . . and fine folk to converse in five or six languages . . . perfection attained at last." Cummings wrote about their imprisonment in *The Enormous Room.*

Christopher Street is the hub of New York's gay community. Walking west, you'll pass the Oscar Wilde Memorial Bookshop (15 Christopher Street), which specializes in gay publications, en route to:

21. **Waverly Place and Christopher Street** (Stonewall Place). The wedge-shaped Georgian Northern Dispensary building dates to 1831; it was so named, because, at the time, this was the north part of the city. Edgar Allan Poe was treated for a head cold here in 1836, the year he came to New York with his 13-year-old bride for whom he would later compose the pain-filled requiems *Annabel Lee* and *Ulalume.*

> *I was a child and she was a child,*
> *In this kingdom by the sea;*
> *But we loved with a love that*
> *was more than love—*
> *I and my Annabel Lee.*

Further west is:

22. **The Lion's Head,** 59 Christopher Street (tel. 929-0670), which has been a writer's bar/media hangout since its inception in 1958 (at this location since 1966). Jessica Lange worked here as a waitress before rising to Hollywood fame. A Lion's Head bartender once described the bar as a place for "writers with a drinking problem," which a customer later amended to a place for "drinkers with a writing problem." Another bartender characterized the clientele as "Irishmen who write like Jews and Jews who drink like Irishmen." When Norman Mailer ran for mayor in the '60s, Joe Flaherty ran his campaign from the bar. And Jack Newfield and Pete Hamill talked Bobby Kennedy into

running for president at the round table in the back. Lion's Head regulars have included newspaper people (Nat Hentoff, Sid Zion, Jimmy Breslin), scores of TV newspeople such as Tony Guida and Linda Ellerby, and actors (Al Pacino, Matthew Broderick, Tim Hutton). The walls are lined with book jackets of regular customers. Stop in for a beer or a bite; the food's pretty good. Open daily except Christmas from noon to 4am.

Note no. 53 Christopher Street, close by. **The Stonewall** was the scene of the Stonewall riots of June, 1969, which launched the lesbian and gay rights movement. The event is commemorated throughout the country every year with gay pride parades. Across the street, in Sheridan Square Park, George Segal's sculptures also honor the gay community.

Make a right on West 4th Street and look for:

23. **238 West 4th Street.** In 1958, Edward Albee wrote his first play, The Zoo Story, at a rickety kitchen table in his apartment here. It took him exactly three weeks. The play was presented at the Provincetown Playhouse in 1960. Albee was the adopted son of a wealthy family and came into a $100,000 trust set up by his grandmother in the 1940s, a fortune in those days.

Turn around and walk back to 10th Street. Make a left to find:

24. **165 West 10th Street.** Theodore Dreiser lived here from 1914 to 1920, during which time he wrote *The "Genius,"* an autobiographically inspired novel. Published in 1915, it was immediately declared obscene and banned by the Society for the Suppression of Vice. New York literati rallied around the issue of freedom of expression for writers. After many court battles, Dreiser—who was championed by H. L. Mencken—managed to get *The "Genius"* back into bookstores in 1923. It was not the first—or the last—time Dreiser tangled with censors. *Sister Carrie,* his first novel, was suppressed because its heroine, "a fallen woman," triumphantly escapes the "wages of sin." And *An American Tragedy* also inspired the wrath of the Mrs. Grundys. During Dreiser's tenancy, Edgar Lee Masters read his *Spoon River* poems at a party here. The building Dreiser lived in was

demolished and replaced by the very unprepossessing two-tone brick structure you see today.

Continue in the same direction, crossing Waverly Place, to:

25. **139 West 10th Street.** Today an Italian restaurant, this was the site, for decades, of a popular Village bar called the Ninth Circle. But it was at a former bar at this location that, in 1954, playwright Edward Albee saw graffiti on a mirror reading, "who's afraid of Virginia Woolf?" and, years later, appropriated it. He recalled the incident in a *Paris Review* interview: "When I started to write the play it cropped up in my mind again. And of course, Who's Afraid of Virginia Woolf means . . . who's afraid of living life without false illusions."

From West 10th Street, cross Greenwich Avenue and walk a block to:

26. **Patchin Place.** This tranquil, tree-shaded cul-de-sac has sheltered many illustrious residents: From 1923 to 1962, e. e. cummings lived at no. 4, where visitors included T. S. Eliot, Ezra Pound, and Dylan Thomas. The highly acclaimed but not widely known Djuna Barnes (literary critics have compared her to James Joyce) lived in a tiny one-room apartment at no. 5. Reclusive and eccentric, she almost never left the premises over a 40-year period, prompting cummings to occasionally shout from his window, "Are you still alive, Djuna?" Barnes once described her early years in New York when she was a successful journalist as "so very, very desperate." She explained her withdrawal from society this way:

"Years ago I used to see people, I had to, I was a newspaperwoman, among other things. And I used to be rather the life of the party. I was rather gay and silly and bright and all that sort of stuff and wasted a lot of time. I used to be invited by people who said, 'Get Djuna for dinner, she's amusing.' So I stopped it."

Among other works, Barnes wrote a memoir called *Life Is Painful, Nasty, & Short . . . In My Case It Has Only Been Nasty* (actually it was also long; she lived to the age of 90); an experimental poetic novel called *Nightwood* (for which T. S. Eliot penned an introduction); and a collection of poetry called *The Book of Repulsive Women.* Three of her one-act plays were produced at the Provincetown Playhouse in 1919 and 1920.

Though they were usually elsewhere, John Reed and Louise Bryant maintained a residence at Patchin Place from 1895 until his death in 1920. It was during this time that he wrote his eyewitness account of the Russian Revolution, *Ten Days That Shook the World.* To avoid interruptions from callers at Patchin Place, Reed rented a room atop a restaurant at 147 West 4th Street to do his writing. Theodore Dreiser and John Masefield are additional past Patchin Place residents, the former in 1895 when he was still an unknown journalist. The gate opens; you can go inside.

Walk east to Sixth Avenue and make a left, then make another left at 11th Street to:

27. **118 West 11th Street.** Theodore Dreiser completed *An American Tragedy* in a no-longer-extant town house here that is today part of P.S. 41.

Walk back to Sixth Avenue and head north, making a left on 13th Street to:

28. **138 West 13th Street.** Max Eastman and other radicals urged revolution in the pages of the *Liberator,* headquartered in this lovely building on a pleasant tree-lined street. The magazine published works by John Reed, as well as Edna St. Vincent Millay, Ernest Hemingway, Elinor Wylie, e. e. cummings (who later became very right-wing and a passionate supporter of Sen. Joseph McCarthy's Communist witch hunts), John Dos Passos, and William Carlos Williams. The *Liberator* (established in 1919) succeeded *The Masses,* an earlier Eastman publication (see Stop 30). And the *Liberator* itself was succeeded by a publication called the *New Masses.*

Further west along the block is:

29. **152 West 13th Street.** Offices of the *Dial,* a major avant-garde literary magazine of the 1920s, occupied this beautiful Greek Revival brick town house. In its earliest incarnation, the magazine dated back to 1840 in Cambridge, Massachusetts, where trascendentalists Margaret Fuller (later literary critic for the *Tribune*) and Ralph Waldo Emerson were its seminal editors. In the '20s, its aim was to offer

"the best of European and American art, experimental and conventional." Contributors included Marianne Moore, Hart Crane, Conrad Aiken, Ezra Pound, Theodore Dreiser (who once wrote an article claiming that American literature had to be crude to be truly American), and artist Marc Chagall. William Carlos Williams savaged the *Dial* in 1921 ("If there is a loonier pack of nitwits in the world than you fellows who are making the *Dial,* they are not advertising it to the world as you are"), but later became a contributor. And T. S. Eliot, who had grumbled "there is far too much in it, and it is all second rate and exceedingly solemn," nevertheless published *The Waste Land* in its pages. In an interview in the *Paris Review* in 1963, one-time editor Marianne Moore (1926–1929) reminisced about her days at the *Dial:* "I think that individuality was the great thing. We were not conforming to anything. We certainly didn't have a policy, except I remember hearing the word 'intensity' very often. A thing must have an 'intensity.' That seemed to be the criterion."

Continue west on 13th Street, and make a left on Seventh Avenue, a right on 12th Street, and then a left to:

30. **91 Greenwich Avenue.** At the beginning of the 20th century, Max Eastman was editor of a radical left-wing literary magazine called *The Masses,* which published, among others, John Reed, Carl Sandburg, Sherwood Anderson, Upton Sinclair, Edgar Lee Masters, e. e. cummings, Walter Lippman, Amy Lowell, and Louis Untermeyer. John Sloan, Stuart Davis, Picasso, and George Bellows provided art for its pages, which a newspaper columnist dismissed thusly:

> *They draw nude women for* The Masses,
> *Thick, fat, ungainly lasses—*
> *How does that help the working classes?*

Reed wrote the magazine's statement of purpose: "To everlastingly attack old systems, old morals, old prejudices." *The Masses* was suppressed by the Justice Department in 1918 because of its opposition to World War I (it called on Woodrow Wilson to repeal the draft and claimed that America's enemy was not Germany but "that 2 percent of the United States that owns 60 percent of all the wealth"). Reed, Eastman, political cartoonist Art Young, and writer/literary critic Floyd Dell were put on trial under the Espionage Act and charged with conspiracy to obstruct recruiting and prevent enlistment. Pacifist Edna St. Vincent Millay read poems to the accused to help pass the time while juries were out. The trials all ended in hung juries. Today the offices of *The Masses* house a video rental store. So much for today's political/cultural scene.

Head east on Greenwich Avenue, make a right on Bank Street, and look for:

31. **5 Bank Street.** In 1913, shortly after the publication of *O Pioneers!,* Willa Cather, age 40, moved to a seven-room, second-floor apartment in a large brick house at this address (today the awning says 1 Bank Street). Here she lived with her companion Edith Lewis and wrote *My Antonia* (the third of a trilogy about immigrants in the U.S.), *Death Comes to the Archbishop,* and several other novels; they're listed on a plaque out front. In 1920, H. L. Mencken called *My Antonia* "the best piece of fiction ever done by a woman in America" (oh, the unconscious male chauvinism of those days). "I know of no novel," said Mencken, "that makes the remote folk of the western farmlands more real than *My Antonia* makes them, and know of none that makes them seem better worth knowing."

When she became successful, Cather rented the apartment above hers and kept it empty to insure perfect quiet. Her Friday afternoon at-homes here were frequented by D. H. Lawrence, among others. Unlike many Village writers of her day, Cather eschewed the radical scene and took little interest in political ferment. Her own favorite writers were Henry James (whom she considered "the perfect writer"), Mark Twain, and Sarah Orne Jewett, the latter a mentor to whom she dedicated *O Pioneers!* It was Jewett who encouraged Cather to abandon journalism and take herself seriously as a novelist.

Take a Break **Ye Waverly Inn,** 16 Bank Street, at Waverly Place (tel. 929-4377), nestles cozily on the lower floor of an 1844 inn. It consists of a warren of rooms with low beamed ceilings, blazing brick fireplaces, and lace-curtained windows. The old carriage courtyard, today an awninged garden patio, provides outdoor seating. The food is traditional American fare such as chicken pot pie, omelets, and meatloaf. Robert de Niro often stuffed himself on Southern fried chicken here to gain weight for *Raging Bull.* And in days of yore, Edna St. Vincent Millay and Robert Frost were frequent customers. The garden is heated in winter. Open daily 11am to 11pm.

From Bank Street start heading down Waverly Place and turn left on Charles Street to find:

32. **15 Charles Street.** Richard Wright owned a mid-19th-century brownstone here from 1945 to 1947, now sadly replaced by a modern apartment building with all the charm of a prison.

Continue in the same direction, and turn left at Greenwich Avenue to:

33. **45 Greenwich Avenue.** William Styron—who came to New York from North Carolina in 1947 to work as a junior editor at McGraw-Hill—moved here in 1951, after a stint in the Marines and the success of his first novel, *Lie Down in Darkness.* Styron originally showed manuscript pages from that novel—begun at age 23—to Hiram Haydn, a Bobbs-Merrill editor whose writing class he was taking at the New School. Haydn told Styron he was too advanced for the class and took an option on the novel.

Continue west on Greenwich Avenue and make a left on Perry Street to reach:

34. **38 Perry Street.** After James Agee graduated from Harvard in 1932, he moved into a basement apartment here, which he occupied for five years. It was during this time that he began writing his Pulitzer Prize–winning autobiographical novel, *A Death in the Family.* The building, which dates to 1845, had a backyard garden and porch. Agee wrote a friend that he was living in "a nice and unusually old house" with "a broad and sheltered back porch, and a large yard with pool, large trees, incipient grass, flower beds and ivy."

Take a Break **Tartine,** 253 West 11th Street, at West 4th Street (tel. 229-2611), is a little gem of an eatery with corner windows (embellished with flower boxes) overlooking charming Village streets and a few café tables out front under an awning. Classic French fare, moderately priced, includes quiches, sandwiches on croissant or brioche, salade niçoise, steak aux poivre, pomme frites, and scrumptious patisseries. Lunch is served weekdays from 11:30am to 4pm, brunch weekends from 10:30am to 4pm.

Continue west on Perry Street, make a right on West 4th Street, and then a left on West 11th Street to:

35. **263 West 11th Street.** After he became successful, Thomas Wolfe and his lover, set designer Aline Bernstein, moved to these elegant digs. Wolfe rhapsodizes over this home (though he places it on 12th Street) in the opening pages of his novel *You Can't Go Home Again*: "its red brick walls, its rooms of noble height and spaciousness, its old dark woods and floors that creaked; and in the magic of the moment it seemed to be enriched and given a profound and lonely dignity by all the human beings it had sheltered in its ninety years." If I lived here, I'd want to go home again and again. The building dates to the 19th century, and its front door and facade are the same as when Wolfe lived here. The brick was cleaned a few years ago.

Continue west on 11th Street to:

36. **The White Horse Tavern,** 567 Hudson Street (tel. **989-3956**), which dates back to 1880. I especially love the front room, with its original 19th-century mahogany bar, oak backbar, and pressed-tin ceiling. Over the decades, it has served everyone from Thomas Wolfe to Joan Didion. The White Horse was a famous literary hangout of the 1950s, when Dan Wolf, founder of the *Village Voice,* and Norman Mailer initiated Sunday afternoon gatherings here. Jack Kerouac, Pete Hamill, Jimmy Breslin, Joe Flaherty, Allen Ginsberg, and James Baldwin were among the attendees. Mailer liked it because, he said, "if you invited people to your house, it was not that easy to get rid of them."

The tavern's most famous tippler was Welsh poet Dylan Thomas, who collapsed a few steps from the door one night (legend has it after gulping down 18 shots of whiskey in less than 20 minutes) and was taken to nearby St. Vincent's Hospital where he died several days later. He was 39 years

GREENWICH VILLAGE LITERARY TOUR PART II

Start: Bleecker Street between La Guardia Place and Thompson Street.

Subway: Take the 6 to Bleecker Street, which lets you out at Bleecker and Lafayette Streets. Walk west on Bleecker.

Finish: 14 West 10th Street.

Time: Approximately 2¹/₂ hours.

Best Time: Any time the weather is conducive to walking.

Like the preceding tour, the walk below concentrates on the people and places that figure prominently in the literary history of the Village. This tour covers an area just east of the route we followed on the other walk; it centers around Washington Square Park, the hub of the Village, where you can follow in the footsteps of Henry James and Edith Wharton.

● ● ● ● ● ● ● ● ● ● ● ● ● ●

Begin at:

1. **145 Bleecker Street,** where James Fenimore Cooper, author of 32 novels—plus a dozen works of nonfiction—lived in 1833. His friend Samuel F. B. Morse (inventor of Morse code and the telegraph, also a noted 19th-century painter and New York University professor) found the house for him.

   Though he is primarily remembered for romantic adventure stories of American frontier, Cooper also wrote political commentary, naval history, sea stories, and a group of novels about the Middle Ages. His father—judge, congressman, and Federalist Party leader William Cooper—founded Cooperstown, New York, the author's childhood home. This was the setting for the author's *Leatherstocking Tales* (the epic of frontiersman Natty Bumppo, written over a period of 19 years, which includes *The Pioneers, The Last of the Mohicans, The Prairie, The Pathfinder,* and *The Deerslayer*). The town is certainly more famous today as the home of the Baseball Hall of Fame. Cooper entered Yale at age 13 (not an uncommon occurrence in the early 19th century) but was expelled in his junior year for pranks, one of them involving the placing of a donkey in a professor's chair. He later wrote rather bitterly of his days at Yale: "There is nothing more vicious than self-righteousness, and the want of charity it engenders." At 17, his aborted college career was followed by a stint in the merchant marine and the navy. His first novel, *Precaution,* was published in 1820. It created no great stir in the literary world, but a second novel focusing on the American Revolution, *The Spy,* appeared a year later and enjoyed vast success, as did his later books.

   Continue west to:

2. **160 Bleecker Street.** This palatial Beaux Arts–style lodging, designed as the Mills House (for men of modest means) by noted architect Ernest Flagg, was the first New York address of Theodore Dreiser in 1895. His rent was 25¢ a night. By the late 1950s it had degenerated into a flophouse, and Art D'Lugoff was able to acquire an inexpensive 40-year lease for his famous jazz club, the now sadly defunct Village Gate. Today a luxury apartment building called the Atrium, it originally contained 1,500 cell-like rooms, many of them overlooking interior garden courtyards.

Across the street is the:

3. **Circle in the Square Theater,** 159 Bleecker Street, founded by Ted Mann and Jose Quintero in 1951 at the site of an abandoned nightclub on Sheridan Square; it moved to Bleecker Street in 1959. It was one of the first arena or "in-the-round" theaters in the United States. Tennessee Williams's *Summer and Smoke* (starring Geraldine Page), Eugene O'Neill's *The Iceman Cometh* (starring Jason Robards, Jr.), Thornton Wilder's *Plays for Bleecker Street,* Truman Capote's *The Grass Harp,* and Jean Genet's *The Balcony* all premiered here. Actors Colleen Dewhurst, Dustin Hoffman, James Earl Jones, Cicely Tyson, Jason Robards, George C. Scott, and Peter Falk honed their craft on the Circle in the Square stage. And Sunday programs (lectures, readings, et. al.) in the early 1950s featured Gore Vidal, Dorothy Parker, Tennessee Williams, Arthur Miller, and many illustrious others. Since 1972 the theater has had an additional stage uptown at 50th Street and Broadway. At both locations, it presents high-quality productions of important plays.

Further west is:

4. **172 Bleecker Street.** Writer James Agee lived in a top floor railroad flat here from 1941 to 1951, after he completed *Let Us Now Praise Famous Men.* Though in the 1960s the book enjoyed a great vogue, it was originally scathingly reviewed and went out of print in 1948 after selling a mere 1,025 copies. Ralph Thompson of *The New York Times* called Agee "arrogant, mannered, precious, gross," and his book "the choicest recent example of how to write self-inspired, self-conscious, and self-indulgent prose." In the *Saturday Review* Selden Rodman opined that Agee's excesses would make the reader "throw down the volume in rage, and curse the author for a confused adolescent, an Ezra Pound in Wolfe's clothing, a shocking snob." *Time* called it "the most distinguished failure of the season." And I'll add my own personal critique: Agee's feverish self-flagellation, guilt, and fawning idealization of the poor makes me not only wish to throw the volume down in a rage but to throw up.

Rallying from critical buffets, during his Bleecker Street tenancy Agee created the screenplay for *The African Queen* and worked as a movie critic for both *Time* and *The*

Nation. He had to move from this walk-up apartment after he suffered a heart attack.

Nearby, on the quintessential Village corner of Bleecker and MacDougal is the:

5. **Café Figaro,** 184–186 Bleecker Street, a Beat-generation haunt. In 1969 Village residents were disheartened to see the Figaro close and in its place arise a sterile-looking Blimpie's. Miraculously, in 1976, the present owner completely restored the Figaro to its earlier appearance, replastering its walls once again with shellacked copies of the French newspaper *Le Figaro.* Having personally whiled away many leisurely hours here over cappuccino and intense conversation in the 1960s, I can vouch for the authenticity of the restoration. If you're here in the morning, stop in for pastries and coffee or an omelet and absorb the atmosphere. It opens at 10:30am Monday through Friday and serves a full prix-fixe brunch Saturdays and Sundays from 10am to 3pm. Weather permitting, it's very pleasant to sit at café tables on the street.

Further along Bleecker, past MacDougal Street:

6. **190 Bleecker Street** was the birthplace of Beat poet Gregory Corso in 1930. Born in the Village; how hip can you get? Unlike other Beat writers who were well educated and in rebellion from middle-class backgrounds, Corso never went beyond sixth grade and spent most of his early life in foster homes, reform schools, and prisons. While Harvard grad William Burroughs was introducing Columbia grads Allen Ginsberg and Jack Kerouac to the hookers and drug addicts of Times Square, Corso was serving a three-year sentence for robbery. Their streetwise hipster demeanor was learned; his came naturally. Kerouac used Corso as the model for his character Raphael Urso in *Desolation Angels,* whom he describes as having "a great mellifluous mind, deep, with amazing images."

Bleecker Street, by the way, was named for a writer, Anthony Bleecker, whose friends included Washington Irving and William Cullen Bryant. The Bleecker family farm occupied this area.

Across the way is:

7. **189 Bleecker Street.** For several decades, beginning in the late 1920s, the San Remo (today Carpo's Cafe), an Italian restaurant at the corner of Bleecker and MacDougal Streets, was a writer's hangout frequented by James Baldwin, William Styron, Jack Kerouac, James Agee, Frank O'Hara, Gregory Corso, Dylan Thomas, William Burroughs, and Allen Ginsberg. Gaunt Village character/poet Max Bodenheim also hung out at the San Remo; author of 14 novels, he sold poems to customers in exchange for food and drink. Though Bodenheim achieved early success with *Replenishing Jessica,* a novel about a nymphomaniac, his life ended tragically; homeless and destitute, he was shot to death in a Bowery flophouse. John Clellon Holmes wrote about the San Remo in his 1952 novel, *Go*—one of the first published works of the Beat generation.

Head north on MacDougal Street to the:

8. **Minetta Tavern,** 113 MacDougal Street, at Minetta Lane (tel. 475-3850), which was a speakeasy called the Black Rabbit during Prohibition. The most unlikely event to take place here in those wild days was the founding of De Witt Wallace's very unbohemian *Reader's Digest* on the premises in 1923; the magazine was published in the basement in its early days. Since 1937, the Minetta has been a simpatico Italian restaurant and meeting place for writers and other creative folk, including Ezra Pound, e. e. cummings, Louis Bromfield, and Ernest Hemingway.

Archetypical Village bohemian Joe Gould—who spent 30 years gathering material for his lifework, a vast never-published book (several thousand pages, scrawled in longhand) called *An Oral History of Our Time*—made it his headquarters. Since most of his vast collection of notebooks disappeared after his death in 1957, no one will ever know whether this voluminous work was a long rant or a masterpiece. The parts that have been found consist mostly of overheard Village conversations, recorded verbatim. A bald and bearded Harvard grad, Gould was nicknamed Professor Seagull, because he would flap his arms and read poetry in what he called the language of a seagull to get people to buy him drinks. His stated credo: "I believe everyone has the right to buy me dinner." He had no fixed address, often sleeping in Bowery flophouses.

The Minetta still evokes the old Village. Walls are covered with photographs and caricatures of famous patrons (about 20 of them are by artist Franz Kline, who did them in exchange for drinks and food), and the rustic pine-paneled back room is adorned with murals of local landmarks. Stop in for a drink or a meal. The Minetta is open daily from noon to midnight serving traditional Italian fare.

Minetta Lane is named for the Minetta Brook that started on 23rd Street and flowed through here en route to the Hudson. The brook still runs underground.

Uptown and across the street stands an 1852 house fronted by twin entrances and a wisteria-covered portico.

9. **130–132 MacDougal Street** belonged to Louisa May Alcott's uncle and, after the Civil War, Alcott lived and worked here. Her best-known work was the autobiographical children's classic *Little Women* (Jo, Amy, Meg, and Beth were based on Alcott and her sisters Abbie, Anna, and Lizzie, respectively). It is believed she wrote *Little Women* at this address. Alcott grew up in Concord, Massachusetts, the daughter of transcendentalist Amos Bronson Alcott. Emerson was a close family friend (his library was at her disposal), and Thoreau taught the young Louisa botany. Briefly a Union hospital nurse in Washington, D.C., during the Civil War (until a case of typhoid fever nearly killed her), Alcott later published a book of letters documenting that time under the title *Hospital Sketches.* Mercury poisoning from the medication left her in fragile health the rest of her life. Henry James called Alcott "The novelist of children . . . the Thackery, the Trollope, of the nursery and schoolroom." And G. K. Chesterton, writing in 1907, grudgingly admitted that "even from a masculine standpoint, the books are very good."

On the other side of the street, just past West 3rd Street, is:

10. **The Provincetown Playhouse,** 133 MacDougal Street (tel. 477-5048), first established in 1915 on a wharf in Provincetown, Massachusetts. Later it moved to this converted stable, where it was managed by Eugene O'Neill through 1927. Founders George Cram "Jig" Cook and his

Greenwich Village Literary Tour Part II

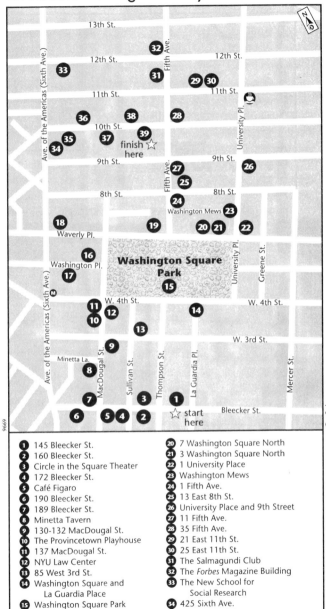

1 145 Bleecker St.
2 160 Bleecker St.
3 Circle in the Square Theater
4 172 Bleecker St.
5 Café Figaro
6 190 Bleecker St.
7 189 Bleecker St.
8 Minetta Tavern
9 130-132 MacDougal St.
10 The Provincetown Playhouse
11 137 MacDougal St.
12 NYU Law Center
13 85 West 3rd St.
14 Washington Square and
   La Guardia Place
15 Washington Square Park
16 75 Washington Place
17 82 Washington Place
18 116 Waverly Place
19 19 Washington Square North
   (Waverly Place)

20 7 Washington Square North
21 3 Washington Square North
22 1 University Place
23 Washington Mews
24 1 Fifth Ave.
25 13 East 8th St.
26 University Place and 9th Street
27 11 Fifth Ave.
28 35 Fifth Ave.
29 21 East 11th St.
30 25 East 11th St.
31 The Salmagundi Club
32 The *Forbes* Magazine Building
33 The New School for
   Social Research
34 425 Sixth Ave.
35 54 West 10th St.
36 45 West 10th St.
37 50 West 10th St.
38 37 West 10th St.
39 14 West 10th St.

wife Susan Glaspell began by producing their own plays on a beachfront porch in Cape Cod. One day an intense young man—the 27-year-old O'Neill, who had arrived in Provincetown with a trunk full of plays—brought a few over to read to Cook and Glaspell. They immediately recognized his genius and were inspired to create a theater dedicated to experimental drama. Many of O'Neill's early plays—*Bound East for Cardiff, The Hairy Ape, The Long Voyage Home, The Emperor Jones,* and *All God's Chillun's Got Wings* (starring the magnificent Paul Robeson), among them—premiered here. The latter play was especially radical for its time, portraying a racially mixed couple; Robeson actually kissed white actress Mary Blair (literary critic Edmund Wilson's wife) on stage, prompting Ku Klux Klan threats and other manifestations of outrage. Nevertheless, the play ran for five months. Robeson later starred in *The Emperor Jones* as well. Other seminal figures in the theater's early days were Max Eastman, Djuna Barnes, Edna Ferber, and John Reed. Edna St. Vincent Millay, whose unlikely life plan was to support herself as a poet by earning her living as an actress, joined in answer to a casting call, snagging the lead in Fred Dell's *An Angel Intrudes,* and Dell himself (their love affair inspired her poems *Weeds* and *Journal*). Millay's own work, *Aria da Capo,* was produced here in 1919. Another notable Provincetown Playhouse production was e. e. cummings' *him,* a play with 21 scenes and 105 characters! Katharine Cornell, Tallulah Bankhead, Bette Davis (who made her stage debut here), and Eva Le Gallienne appeared on the Provincetown stage in its early years. The theater was a great success, and O'Neill's plays went on to Broadway. But instead of basking in their popularity, Cook and Glaspell, ever the rebels, disbanded the company and moved on to Greece; they were convinced that acceptance by the establishment signaled their failure as revolutionary artists. Though this is still an off-Broadway stage, the Provincetown Players gave their last performance on December 14, 1929.

Next door is:

11. **137 MacDougal Street.** Jack London, Upton Sinclair, Vachel Lindsay, Louis Untermeyer, Max Eastman, Theodore Dreiser, Lincoln Steffens, and Sinclair Lewis hashed over

life theories at the Liberal Club, "A Meeting Place for Those Interested in New Ideas," founded in 1913 on the second floor of a house at this address. Margaret Sanger lectured the club on birth control, Sherwood Anderson read his plays, an on-premises organization called Heterodoxy worked to promote feminist causes, and cubist art was displayed on the walls. The group raised money by staging wild all-night revels dubbed "Pagan Routs" by Fred Dell. Downstairs were Polly's Restaurant (run by anarchists Polly Holladay and Hippolyte Havel) and the radical Washington Square Book Shop from which Liberal Club members more often borrowed than bought, returning their books used, dog-eared and in a dubious condition of saleability. Holladay, being a staunch anarchist, would not even join the Liberal Club, which, however bohemian, was still an "organization." The apopleptic Havel, who was on the editorial board of *The Masses* (see Walking Tour 5, Stop 30), once shouted out at a meeting where fellow members were voting on which contributions to accept: "Bourgeois pigs! Voting! Voting on poetry! Poetry is something from the soul! You can't vote on poetry!" When Floyd Dell pointed out to Havel that he had previously participated in a similar process making editorial selections for Emma Goldman's radical magazine, *Mother Earth,* Havel shot back, "Yes, but we didn't abide by the results!" Hugo Kalmar, a character in O'Neill's *The Iceman Cometh,* is purportedly based on Havel. In a previous incarnation, this building was the home of Nathaniel Currier (of Currier & Ives).

Across MacDougal Street stands the:

12. **NYU Law Center,** occupying a city block bounded by West 3rd, MacDougal, Sullivan, and West 4th Streets. It is on the site of a previous building at 42 Washington Square where Lincoln Steffens lived. Another famed resident of no. 42—writer, war correspondent, and later Communist, John Reed (portrayed by Warren Beatty in the movie *Reds*)—wrote about the building in a lengthy, youthful paean titled *The Day in Bohemia or Life Among the Artists.* Dedicated to his friend Steffens, it includes the lines:

> *But nobody questions your morals,*
> *And nobody asks for the rent,*

> *There's no one to pry, if we're tight, you and I,*
> *Or demand how our evenings are spent.*
> *The furniture's ancient but plenty,*
> *The linen is spotless and fair,*
> *O life is a joy to a broth of a boy*
> *At Forty-two Washington Square!*

Steffens, like Reed, was a radical. After visiting post-revolutionary Russia in 1919, he proclaimed, "I have seen the future, and it works." Eugene O'Neill also lived in this building during World War I, when he was having an affair with Louise Bryant, John Reed's lover (Diane Keaton in the movie). That affair, by the way, inspired O'Neill's 1927 drama, *Strange Interlude.*

The Law Center additionally encompasses 144 MacDougal Street, where, in 1942, Anaïs Nin rented a studio, installed a printing press, and published a novel, *Winter of Artifice,* and a collection of stories titled *Under a Glass Bell,* as well as a book of Max Ernst drawings.

Head back the way you came on MacDougal Street and make a left on West 3rd Street to reach:

13. **85 West 3rd Street.** Edgar Allan Poe lived on the third floor (his window is in the right-hand corner if you care to gaze) of this very unusual-looking building in 1845. He wrote *Facts in the Case of M. Valdemar* here, and *The Raven* was published during his tenancy. Later the building housed a gay bar called the Gold Bug, named for a Poe story. Today, it's part of NYU Law School, and the current residents claim Poe's rooms are haunted. Walt Whitman, whose *Art-Music and Heart Music* Poe had published when he was editor and part owner of the *Broadway Journal,* described the poet as "very kindly and human, but subdued, perhaps a little jaded."

Continue in the same direction to La Guardia Place and make a left to:

14. **Washington Square and La Guardia Place.** NYU's Loeb Student Center was once Madame Branchard's Rooming House, where tenants, at various times, included Stephen Crane, O. Henry, Willa Cather, John Dos Passos, Pierre

Matisse, Upton Sinclair, and Theodore Dreiser. Because of its many illustrious occupants—described in the above-mentioned poem by John Reed (see Stop 12) as:

> . . . *Inglorious Miltons by the score—*
> *Mute Wagners—Rembrandts, ten or more—*
> *And Rodins . . . one to every floor . . .*

—its seedy studios were known as the "genius houses." Cather's short story, *Coming, Aphrodite!* is set here.

Across the street is:

15. **Washington Square Park.** What is today Washington Square Park, the hub of the Village, began as a swamp frequented largely by duck hunters. Minetta Brook meandered through it. In the 18th and early 19th centuries it was a potter's field (over 10,000 people are buried under the park) and an execution site; some of the trees still standing were used as gallows. The park was dedicated in 1826, and elegant residential dwellings—some of which have survived NYU's cannibalization of the neighborhood—went up around the square. Rather than the center of Bohemia which it later became, it was the citadel of stifling patrician gentility so evocatively depicted in the novels of Edith Wharton. She defined Washington Square society as "a little 'set' with its private catch-words, observances and amusements" indifferent to "anything outside its charmed circle."

The beautiful white marble Memorial Arch at the Fifth Avenue entrance—which in 1892 replaced a wooden arch erected in 1889 to commemorate the centenary of Washington's inauguration—was designed by Stanford White. One night in 1917, a group of Liberal Club pranksters (see Stop 11) climbed the Washington Square Arch, fired cap guns, and proclaimed the "independent republic of Greenwich Village," a Utopia dedicated to "socialism, sex, poetry, conversation, dawn-greeting, anything—so long as it is taboo in the Middle West." Today, Washington Square Park would probably surpass any of this group's most cherished anarchist fantasies and might even lead them to question the philosophy altogether.

Walk through the park and exit on the west side to:

16. **75 Washington Place.** A restaurant called Marta's at this site was a favorite in the 1920s of Elinor Wylie, John Dos Passos, and other writers. The building dates to the mid-1800s. In 1991, Marta's became an Italian restaurant called Stella.

    Continue in the same direction. Across the street is:

17. **82 Washington Place,** residence from 1908 to 1912 of Willa Cather, whose books celebrated pioneer life and the beauty of her native Nebraska landscape. Cather came to New York in 1906 at the age of 31 to work at the prestigious *McClure's* magazine and rose to the position of managing editor before resigning to write full-time. As her career advanced, and she found herself besieged with requests for lectures and interviews, Cather became almost reclusive and fiercely protective of her privacy. "In this country," she complained, "a writer has to hide and lie and almost steal in order to get time to work in—and peace of mind to work with. . . . If we lecture, we get a little more owlish and self-satisfied all the time. We hate it at first, if we are decently modest, but in the end we fall in love with the sound of our own voice. There is something insidious about it, destructive to one's finer feelings. . . . It's especially destructive to writers, ever so much worse than alchohol, takes their edge off."

    A later resident (in 1945) was Richard Wright. Band leader John Philip Sousa owned the beautiful 1839 building next door (no. 80).

    Make a right on Sixth Avenue, then another on Waverly Place to find:

18. **116 Waverly Place.** In the 1840s, poet Anne Charlotte Lynch presided over salons here in a parlor with two blazing fireplaces. The current building is of later vintage, dating to 1891. William Cullen Bryant, Horace Greeley, Margaret Fuller, poet Fitz-Greene Halleck (whose statue is among the literary greats along Central Park's Mall), and Herman Melville were frequent guests, and Poe read his latest poem, *The Raven,* to assembled literati. Waverly Place, by the way, was named in 1833 for Sir Walter Scott's novel, *Waverley.*

    Continue walking east. When you get to the northwest corner of the park, note the towering English elm; it was a hanging tree when the park was an execution ground. Opposite the park once stood:

19. **19 Washington Square North (Waverly Place).**
Henry James's grandmother, Elizabeth Walsh, lived at this now-defunct address. (The no. 19 that exists today is a different house, the numbering system having changed since James's day.) Young Henry spent much time at her house— the inspiration for his novel *Washington Square,* which was later made into a movie called *The Heiress* starring Olivia de Havilland. In 1875, James moved to Europe (eventually becoming a British citizen), where he met with Flaubert, Turgenev, and other noted literary figures and wrote about the dilemmas of Americans abroad. James's distinguished family included his philosopher/theologian father, Henry, Sr., and brother William, author of *Varieties of Religious Experience.* Novelist Louis Auchincloss described the Jameses as "a deeply congenial family of inherited means and large ideas whose generations were united by a love of the arts and sciences."

Further east is:

20. **7 Washington Square North,** where Edith Wharton, age 20, and her mother lived in 1882. A wealthy aristocrat, born Edith Jones, Wharton maintained a close friendship with Henry James, and, like him, left New York's stultifying upper-class social scene for Europe (Paris) in 1910, where she wrote the Pulitzer Prize–winning *The Age of Innocence.* Both she and James were immensely popular in Europe, deluged with invitations (James once admitted to accepting 107 dinner invitations in a single year). Wharton wrote almost a book a year her entire adult life, while also finding time to feed French and Belgian refugees during World War I and take charge of 600 Belgian orphans. For these efforts she was awarded the Legion of Honor by the French government in 1915. No. 7 was also once the home of Alexander Hamilton.

Nearby is:

21. **3 Washington Square North** (today the NYU School of Social Work). Critic Edmund Wilson moved to the Village after he graduated from Princeton and became managing editor of the *New Republic.* He lived in this house

from 1921 to 1923. Another resident, John Dos Passos, wrote *Manhattan Transfer* here. Dos Passos, a fiery New York radical in the 1920s, became disillusioned with Communism after journeying to Spain with Hemingway during the Spanish Civil War. He was appalled that the Marxist-backed Republicans executed his friend Jose Robles, himself a Republican supporter. The incident—which also caused a break between Dos Passos and Hemingway when the latter refused to challenge the integrity of the Republican cause—was the basis of Dos Passos' next novel, *Adventures of a Young Man* (1939). His books thereafter also demonstrated a marked shift to the right. In the 1940s, Dos Passos returned to his native Virginia.

Make a left at University Place to find:

22. **1 University Place.** In the early 1920s, poet/novelist Elinor Wylie lived in this building, where she entertained Edmund Wilson, John Dos Passos, and others. She worked at *Vanity Fair* as poetry editor. Stephen Vincent Benét, recalling the advent of Wylie's first book of verses, *Nets to Catch the Wind,* rhapsodized: "Genius comes among us in many ways, but sometimes as suddenly and sharply as a new star. . . . It was so with Elinor Wylie . . . the usual critical adjectives reserved for first books of verse simply did not apply. It was not 'promising' or 'interesting' or 'creditable'—it was the work of a scrupulous and inimitable artist."

After Edmund Wilson married actress Mary Blair in 1923, they, too, moved to 1 University Place. The current building at this address dates to 1929.

Cross the street and turn left into:

23. **Washington Mews.** This picturesque 19th-century cobblestoned street, lined with vine-covered two-story buildings (converted stables and carriage houses constructed to serve posh Washington Square town houses), has had several famous residents, among them John Dos Passos, artist Edward Hopper (no. 14A), and Sherwood Anderson (no. 54). The latter building dates to 1834.

Continue to the end of Washington Mews, and then turn right to look for:

24. **1 Fifth Avenue.** Poet Sara Teasdale lived in this building from 1931 until 1933, when she committed suicide by overdosing on barbiturates.

     Continue uptown on Fifth Avenue, turning right at 8th Street to find:

25. **13 East 8th Street.** Thomas Wolfe lived here in a converted cold-water sweatshop with his mistress, stage designer Aline Bernstein. It was at this address that he began working on *Look Homeward, Angel.* His first novel, it so barely disguised residents of his hometown, Asheville, North Carolina, that one local lady who had known Wolfe all his life was moved to write him, "Sir: You are a son of a bitch." A big, shaggy man (at 6 feet, 4 inches, he sometimes used the top of his refrigerator for a desk), Wolfe produced long, rambling manuscripts that always required the editorial expertise of Maxwell Perkins (who also edited Hemingway and Fitzgerald). Under Perkins's guidance, several hundred pages were cut from the original manuscript of *Look Homeward, Angel.* Today the building he lived in is replaced by a food shop, but across the street, between University Place and Fifth Avenue, there are still many beautiful old buildings that will give you the flavor of the street in Wolfe's time.

     Continue in the same direction, and make a left at University Place to the intersection of:

26. **University Place and 9th Street.** The café at the Lafayette Hotel on this southeast corner was a very popular gathering spot for writers, artists, and bohemians in the early 1920s. Today it is the Knickerbocker Bar & Grill (tel. 228-8490), a comfortable wood-paneled restaurant and jazz club that still attracts an interesting clientele including writers (Jack Newfield, E. L. Doctorow, Erica Jong, Sidney Zion, Christopher Cerf) and actors (Richard Gere, F. Murray Abraham, Susan Sarandon, Tim Robbins). Harry Connick, Jr., got his start playing piano at the Knickerbocker. And of even greater historic interest: Charles Lindbergh signed the contract for his transatlantic flight at the bar here. The restaurant is open daily for lunch/brunch from 11:45am; an eclectic menu offers entrées ranging from pasta dishes to

bangers and mash to Southwestern paella. Do consider eating here; Knickerbocker's is rather elegant, with white-linened tables and seating in tufted-leather booths. The à la carte menu is a little pricey, but you can enjoy a prix-fixe brunch daily for about $10.

Turn left on 9th Street, and make a left at Fifth Avenue. Just downtown is:

27. **11 Fifth Avenue.** Today the block-long Brevoort Apartments encompass several past literary addresses, including the old Brevoort Hotel that stood on the northeast corner of Fifth Avenue and 8th Street. Noel Coward and his mother lived at the Brevoort in the 1920s. The hotel's basement café was frequented by Isadora Duncan, Lincoln Steffens, John Reed, Emma Goldman, Walter Lippman, Theodore Dreiser, Eugene O'Neill, and Edna St. Vincent Millay. Both Nathanael West and James T. Farrell lived at the Brevoort from 1935 to 1936, the latter while writing *Studs Lonigan.*

Also encompassed in the Brevoort Apartments, and very sadly demolished, was a majestic neo-Gothic brownstone designed by noted architect James Renwick, Jr., for himself in 1851. Mark Twain purchased it in 1904. There Twain wrote and received visitors while prone in a gigantic Italianate bed.

And Mable Dodge, a lover of John Reed (see Stop 12) and a passionate advocate of myriad causes, hosted a popular salon in a decaying mansion at 23 Fifth Avenue (on the corner of 9th Street) in 1913. Each week the meeting had a different theme for discussion—psychoanalysis, birth control (Margaret Sanger lectured), free love, the unemployed, and so on. The air was always "vibrant with intellectual excitement and electrical with the appearance of new ideas and dawning changes." Marsden Hartley and John Marin talked about theories of modern art; the avant-garde Armory Show of 1913—showcasing the works of such then-controversial artists as Matisse, Picasso, Duchamp, and Braque—was conceived in Dodge's drawing room. Emma Goldman preached anarchy, and John Reed organized everyone in aid of striking workers. The guest list comprised all of the basement café crowd described above.

Turn around and continue north along Fifth Avenue to:

28. **35 Fifth Avenue.** In 1927, Willa Cather moved to the no-longer-extant Grosvenor Hotel at 35 Fifth Avenue (today an NYU student residence) after her beloved Bank Street apartment was demolished. What bothered her most about the change of residences was the disruption to her work. Cather spoke about her writing routine in a 1921 interview in the *Bookman:* "I work from two and a half to three hours a day. I don't hold myself to longer hours; if I did, I wouldn't gain by it. The only reason I write is because it interests me more than any other activity I've ever found. . . . If I made a chore of it, my enthusiasm would die. I make it an adventure every day. I get more entertainment from it than any I could buy, except the privilege of hearing a few great musicians and singers. To listen to them interests me as much as a good morning's work."

Continue uptown on Fifth Avenue, and make a right on 11th Street. The handsome ivied town house at:

29. **21 East 11th Street** was the residence of Mary Cadwaller Jones, who was married to Edith Wharton's brother. Her home was the setting of literary salons; Henry Adams, Theodore Roosevelt, Augustus Saint-Gaudens, and John Singer Sargent often came to lunch, and Henry James was a houseguest when he visited America from Europe.

Just east stands:

30. **25 East 11th Street.** The unhappy and sexually confused poet Hart Crane lived here for a short time. Crane was born in 1899 with "a toe in the 19th century." His parents' marriage was a miserably unhappy one, and his mother, an artistic beauty, subject to depression, concentrated her aesthetic energies on her son—giving him music and dancing lessons, taking him to art galleries, and providing him with every kind of children's book and classic. He was his mother's confidant, comforting her as she lay in bed, depressed, sobbing, and railing bitterly against her husband, a successful businessman. The adolescent Crane was her companion; together they traveled across the United States, to Canada and Cuba. Though their travels kept him out of school (he never even finished high school), Crane was a voracious reader—brilliantly self-educated. By the time

he was 17, his poetry had been published in prestigious New York magazines and Nobel Prize–winning Indian poet Rabindranath Tagore had been so impressed by the young man's writing that he arranged to meet him when visiting Cleveland. When Crane, still in his teens, moved to New York, he wrote his mother: "I think it's time you realized that for the last eight years my youth has been a rather bloody battleground for yours and father's sex life and troubles." This brief rebellion notwithstanding, he would run to her side when beckoned time and again. In the next few years his life was spent alternately in New York (where, for a while, he worked as an advertising copywriter at J. Walter Thompson), Cleveland, California, and Europe. In 1923, he lived in Woodstock with novelist William Slater Brown (see Tour 5, Stop 20). These meanderings, marked for the most part by grinding poverty, were punctuated by visits to his ever more desperate mother, who once threatened to reveal his homosexuality to his father if he left her side. Crane's problems were compounded by alcoholism; periods of moderate social drinking alternated with monumental, often violent, binges, some of them leading to incarceration. It was during such a binge that, returning by ship from Mexico, Crane made sexual advances to a crew member, was badly beaten up, and jumped to his death into the Gulf of Mexico.

Take a Break **Dean & Deluca,** 75 University Place, at 11th Street (tel. 473-1908), offers superior light fare—pastries, croissants, ham and brie sandwiches on baguette, pasta salads—in a pristinely charming setting, usually enhanced by classical music. Be sure to note the gorgeous plasterwork ceiling. Open Monday through Thursday from 8am to 10pm, Fridays and Saturdays from 8am to 11pm, and Sundays from 9am to 8pm.

This address is also a stop on the tour. When Thomas Wolfe graduated from Harvard in 1923, he came to New York to teach at NYU and lived at the Hotel Albert (depicted as the Hotel Leopold in his novel *Of Time and the River*) at this address. Today the Albert Apartments occupy the site.

Double back on 11th Street toward Fifth Avenue and make a right en route to:

31. **The Salmagundi Club,** 47 Fifth Avenue, which began as an artist's club in 1871 and was originally located at 596 Broadway. The name comes from the *Salmagundi* papers, in which Washington Irving mocked his fellow New Yorkers and first used the term "Gotham" to describe the city. "Salmagundi," which means "a stew of many ingredients," was thought an appropriate term to describe the club's diverse membership—painters, sculptors, writers, and musicians. The club moved to this mid-19th-century brownstone mansion in 1917. Theodore Dreiser lived at the Salmagundi in 1897 (when it was at 14 West 12th Street, today the First Presbyterian Church across the street) and probably wrote *Sister Carrie* there, a work based on the experiences of his own sister, Emma.

    Cross 12th Street. At the northwest corner is:

32. **The *Forbes* Magazine Building,** 60–62 Fifth Avenue, housing many interesting exhibits from the varied collections of the late Malcolm Forbes, famous as a frequent Liz Taylor escort and as a financier. On display are hundreds of ship models, thousands of military miniatures, exquisite Fabergé eggs and other *objets d'art* (clocks, cigarette boxes, jewelry, ashtrays, picture frames, paper knives) fashioned for the Czars, and changing exhibits and art shows. Admission is free. The galleries are open Tuesday through Saturday from 10am to 4pm. The Fabergé collection especially merits a look.

    Make a left on 12th Street and you'll see.

33. **The New School for Social Research,** 66 West 12th Street, which was founded in 1919. In the 1930s it became a "University in Exile" for intelligentsia fleeing Nazi Germany. Many great writers have taught or lectured in its classrooms over the decades—William Styron, Joseph Heller, Edward Albee, W. H. Auden, Robert Frost, Nadine Gordimer, Max Lerner, Maya Angelou, Joyce Carol Oates, Arthur Miller, I. B. Singer, Susan Sontag, and numerous others.

    Architecturally, this street between Fifth and Sixth Avenues is a delight. Turn left on Sixth to:

34. **425 Sixth Avenue.** The turreted red-brick and granite Victorian-Gothic castle at this corner houses the Jefferson

Market Library, built as a courthouse in 1877 and named for Thomas Jefferson. Topped by a lofty clock/bell tower (originally intended as a fire lookout), with traceried and stained-glass windows, gables, and steeply sloping roofs, the building was inspired by a Bavarian castle. In the 1880s, architects voted it one of the 10 most beautiful buildings in America. Through the early 20th century, the surrounding area comprised a market where Willa Cather used to shop for produce.

Now turn left into 10th Street, another block filled with stunning buildings, where you'll see:

35. **54 West 10th Street.** Poet Hart Crane lived in this 1839 house in 1917; he paid $6 a week for rent. He was just 18 years old at the time but already published. Crane was a romantic visionary and lyric poet whose writings, filled with private symbolism, have been compared to Blake and Baudelaire. Literary critic Malcolm Cowley called him a poet of "ecstasy or frenzy or intoxication."

Across the street is:

36. **45 West 10th Street.** On the site of what is today a 1950s apartment building once stood the home of Kahlil Gibran, whose work, *The Prophet*, was the rage in the 1960s and read at many a hippie wedding. Somehow, I can't imagine him managing to compose such sentiments in this present edifice.

Nearby is:

37. **50 West 10th Street.** After his great success with *Who's Afraid of Virginia Woolf*, playwright Edward Albee bought this late-19th-century converted carriage house in the early 1960s. It's a gem of a building, with exquisite highly polished wooden carriage doors. Albee wrote *Tiny Alice* and *A Delicate Balance* here, the latter a Pulitzer Prize winner. In 1994, he won a second Pulitzer Prize for *Three Tall Women*.

Now look for:

38. **37 West 10th Street.** Sinclair Lewis, already a famous writer by the mid-1920s, lived in this early-19th-century house with his wife, journalist Dorothy Thompson, from 1928 to 1929. Lewis fell in love with the recently divorced Thompson at first sight in 1927, and immediately proposed

to her. Once, when asked to speak at a dinner party he stood up and said, "Dorothy, will you marry me?" and resumed his seat. Lewis later followed her to Russia and all over Europe until she accepted his proposal. It's a romantic story, though the marriage did end in divorce.

Our final stop is:

39. **14 West 10th Street.** When Mark Twain came to New York at the turn of the century (at the age of 65), he lived in this gorgeous 1855 mansion. A greatly successful writer, he entertained lavishly. Born Samuel Langhorne Clemens, Twain, a one-time riverboat captain, took his pseudonym from a river calling that warned of shallow waters ("mark twain" means "by the mark two fathoms"). Twain was famous for witticisms such as "How lucky Adam was. He knew when he said a good thing, nobody had said it before."

MIDTOWN

Start: Grand Central Terminal.

Subway: Take the 4, 5, 6, or the shuttle to 42nd Street/Grand Central.

Finish: The Plaza Hotel.

Time: Approximately 4 hours, not counting time for browsing in shops and galleries.

Best Time: Weekdays, when Midtown is bustling but the attractions aren't packed as they tend to be on weekends.

Worst Time: Rush hour (weekdays from 8:30 to 9:30am and from 4:30 to 6pm).

If there's an area that unmistakably defines New York in the popular imagination, it's Midtown. Concentrated here are dozens of the towering skycrapers that are so closely identified with the city and its skyline; as you walk past them, craning your neck upward in awe, you'll be jostled by the crowds of office workers who occupy these mammoth edifices. Lining Fifth Avenue and 57th Street are the blue-chip art galleries, high-toned boutiques, and chic department stores that make New York the consumer capital of the world. Midtown is Manhattan at its most glamorous.

If you're a first-time visitor with only enough time to take one of the tours in this book, this is the one to choose, since it takes in many of the city's top attractions.

• • • • • • • • • • • • • • • • •

From the subway platform, follow the Metro North signs to the main concourse of:

1. **Grand Central Terminal.** Commodore Vanderbilt himself named the place "Grand Central" in the 1860s, notwithstanding the fact that it was then out in the boondocks. The original station underwent more or less continuous alterations until the present structure replaced it in 1913. It's an engineering tour de force, combining subways, surface streets, pedestrian malls, underground shopping concourses, and 48 pairs of railroad tracks together with attendant platforms and concourses into one smoothly functioning organism.

   The main concourse is perfectly breathtaking. It's one of America's most impressive interior spaces, with gleaming marble floors, sweeping staircases, and a blue vaulted ceiling soaring 125 feet high on which the constellations are traced and highlighted by twinkling electric stars.

   When a developer announced plans to place a huge tower over the concourse in the 1970s, preservationists came to the rescue, with Jackie Onassis leading the charge. The terminal's design survived intact after a series of legal challenges that went all the way to the Supreme Court and resulted in a 1978 decision that upheld the validity of New York City's landmarks laws.

   On the main concourse is a gift shop of the New York Transit Museum that's full of subway souvenirs, maps, and unique gifts. The shop is open Monday through Friday from 8am to 8pm, Saturdays from 10am to 4pm.

   Take a Break There are numerous spots in Grand Central where you can pick up coffee, a muffin, or a sandwich to fortify yourself for the tour, including **Zaro's Bread Basket, Hot & Crusty,** or **Häagen Dazs.**

   For something more substantial, head downstairs from the main concourse to the **Oyster Bar,** where first-rate seafood is served Monday through Friday from 11:30am to 9:30pm. You might take a seat at the counter for an appetizer of fried oysters, New Zealand greenlip mussels in Dijon sauce, or New England clam chowder. Full meals, including the catch of the day, are available in the dining room. A large dessert menu features key lime pie and crème brûlée, and a wine bar offers a large selection of wines by the glass.

Leave the main concourse via the 42nd Street exit and turn right. After you've taken a few steps, look up. Looming over you is the sleek art deco:

2. **Chrysler Building.** At 1,048 feet, it reigned briefly as the tallest building in the world—until the Empire State Building came along. Huge winged radiator caps mark the base of the tower, and above it, the building's spire creates one of the most beautiful and distinctive features of the Manhattan skyline. You'll get a better view of it later in the tour.

Head west along 42nd Street. Make a left onto Fifth Avenue, where the:

3. **New York Public Library** sits in splendor, resembling a Greek temple with rows of Corinthian columns. Completed in 1911, this Beaux Arts palace, one of the greatest research libraries in the world, cost more than $9 million to construct, and President Taft himself attended the dedication ceremony.

Climb up the broad stone steps in front, which are guarded by twin stone lions named Patience and Fortitude. In warm weather, street performers entertain crowds at lunchtime, and cafés on either side of the grounds offer umbrella tables.

On either side of the main entrance are fountains marked by classical statuary. On the left, seated on a winged Pegasus, is a woman who symbolizes Beauty; on the right is Truth, depicted as a balding man, who sits under the inscription "But Above All Things, Truth Beareth Away the Victory." Also on the entrance stairs are two immense stone vases; take a closer look and note the tragic and comic masks just below the lips.

It's well worth exploring the interior, which contains manuscripts, maps, journals, prints, and more than 38 million volumes occupying 80 miles of bookshelves. There's an information desk just inside the lobby where you can sign up for tours (offered at 11am and 2pm). The staff can point you to the library's current exhibits, its wonderful bookstore and gift shop, and to the main reading room, a magnificent space extending the entire block-long length of the building. The library is open on Monday, Thursday, Friday, and Saturday from 10am to 6pm; on Tuesday and Wednesday from 11am to 7:30pm; closed on Sundays.

As you leave the library grounds, you'll pass a flagpole with an elaborate bronze base; note the turtles poking their heads out from each of the four corners. Start heading uptown on the west side of Fifth Avenue, and look up and to your right as you cross 42nd Street—you'll get a wonderful perspective on the Chrysler Building.

Continue north for two blocks to 44th Street, where you'll turn left. On the north side of 44th, at no. 27, is the **Harvard Club,** designed by McKim, Mead, and White in 1894 in an architectural style that was favored at Harvard in the 1800s. The "Veritas" coat of arms tops the building.

Continue along 44th Street. Near Sixth Avenue stands one of New York's most famous literary landmarks:

4. **The Algonquin Hotel.** H. L. Mencken, a Baltimore resident, began staying at the Algonquin on his frequent business trips to New York after he became the editor of *Smart Set* in 1914. Under Mencken's stewardship, the magazine published the early works of Eugene O'Neill, James Joyce, and F. Scott Fitzgerald, and Mencken's columns made him one of the preeminent voices in American literary criticism. Nonetheless, Mencken detested the city and remained unimpressed by its young bohemian writers ("The Village literati are scum," he pronounced).

As *Smart Set* faded from influence in the 1920s, *Vanity Fair* began to take its place, counting Edna St. Vincent Millay, Elinor Wylie, and Theodore Dreiser among its contributors. In its offices at 19 West 44th Street, Dorothy Parker, Robert Benchley, and Robert Sherwood served on the editorial staff. They began hanging out in the Algonquin, and soon their gatherings grew into the famous "Round Table," which also included Alexander Woollcott (drama critic for the *New York Times*), George S. Kaufman, Franklin Adams (columnist for the *New York World*), and Edna

Ferber. The group became famous for its witty, acerbic commentary on theater, literature, and the social scene, though Dorothy Parker herself played down its importance: "The Round Table was just a lot of people telling jokes and telling each other how good they were."

One of the regulars, Harold Ross, took it into his head to start a magazine that would incorporate the group's sophisticated, satirical outlook, and rounded up investors to begin publication of *The New Yorker*, with offices set up nearby at 25 West 45th Street. The first few issues were extremely uneven, but within a couple of years E. B. White and James Thurber had been added to the staff and were reshaping the magazine into one of the most prestigious publications in the country.

Even after the Round Table stopped gathering at the hotel, the Algonquin continued to count famous writers among its guests, including Gertude Stein and her companion Alice B. Toklas, F. Scott Fitzgerald, and William Faulkner, who wrote the acceptance speech for his 1949 Nobel Prize on Algonquin stationery.

To further soak up this hotel's genteel ambience, consider having lunch or weekend brunch in the Rose Room. Or ensconce yourself in a comfortable sofa in the lobby lounge for cocktails. Weekdays, *New Yorker* writers frequently conduct interviews in the latter setting.

Just across the street from the Algonquin, but light years away in style and design, is the **Royalton.** Poke your head inside and take a look—the whimsically futuristic decor, created by Philippe Starck, has to be seen to be believed.

Retrace your steps back to Fifth Avenue and head north. Take a detour to your left when you reach 47th Street. This block, between Fifth and Sixth Avenues, is the Diamond District, where millions of dollars' worth of gems are traded every day. The business hustle on this block makes an unlikely setting for another literary sight, the:

5. **Gotham Book Mart,** on the north side at 41 West 47th Street. Founded in 1920 on West 45th Street, the store moved to 47th Street in 1923. A group of writers known as the Three Hours for Lunch Club began meeting in the bookstore at midday, eating out in the garden; its members

included Christopher Morley, Buckminster Fuller, and William Rose Benét.

H. L. Mencken and his friend Theodore Dreiser once stopped in, and, delighted to find some of their own works in stock, began to scribble dedications on many of the books, including the Bible, which they signed "With the compliments of the authors."

The store has hosted countless book publication parties, and continues to do so today. Over the years the list of writers toasted here has included Dylan Thomas, Katherine Anne Porter, William Carlos Williams, W. H. Auden, Marianne Moore, Joyce Carol Oates, and Tennessee Williams. The most famous such gathering was the 1939 "wake" held to celebrate the publication of James Joyce's *Finnegans Wake.* In 1947, the store became headquarters of the James Joyce Society, whose first membership was purchased by T. S. Eliot.

Owner Frances Steloff (who died in 1989 at the age of 101) was known for lending a hand to perennially cash-strapped artists such as Henry Miller and John Dos Passos (even Martha Graham borrowed $1,000 to stage her first dance performance). This tradition grew into the Writers' Emergency Fund, which still offers loans to struggling writers.

Head back to Fifth Avenue and continue uptown toward 49th Street. On the right side of the avenue stands one of New York's most famous department stores, Saks Fifth Avenue. Immediately opposite Saks, head west into the promenade of:

6. **Rockefeller Center,** one of the most handsome urban complexes in New York. It encompasses 24 acres and 19 skyscrapers, extending from 47th to 52nd Streets between Fifth and Sixth Avenues. People scoffed at John D. Rockefeller in 1929 when he unveiled plans to build this "city within a city," since it was so far removed from what was then the commercial heart of New York. But Rockefeller proved all the critics wrong. His complex remade the map, drawing business uptown and setting the standard for future civic projects by incorporating public art and open spaces.

Stroll west past the Channel Gardens, with their beautiful plantings, to Rockefeller Center's famous skating rink. In the summer, this area becomes an outdoor café; in cooler months, it's packed with skaters gliding along the ice while music wafts through the air and the trees surrounding the rink twinkle with tiny lights. Around the rink flutter the flags of many nations. Each holiday season a giant Christmas tree stands here, towering over the promenade. Paul Manship's massive *Prometheus* sits above the skating rink, beneath a quote from Aeschylus.

Take a look inside the lobby of 30 Rockefeller Plaza, once the RCA Building and now renamed the GE Building. Above the black marble floors and walls are monumental sepia-toned murals by José Maria Sert. Originally, a highly political mural by Diego Rivera faced the building's front door and caused a tiff between Rivera and Rockefeller. Rather than giving in to Rockefeller's wish that he remove an image of Lenin hovering over a tableau of rich people playing cards, Rivera insisted that the mural be destroyed. The Rockefellers willingly obliged. The building, a stunning example of art deco architecture, was featured in the movie *Quiz Show*.

Just to the left of 30 Rockefeller Plaza, head west on 49th Street to Sixth Avenue. You'll pass the entrance to NBC Studios (where *Late Night with David Letterman* was taped for many years before Letterman defected to CBS) and to the Rainbow Room, one of New York's most glamorous supper clubs.

When you reach Sixth Avenue, turn right and head uptown. A building boom in the 1960s and 1970s transformed this area into an astonishing canyon of 50-story glass skyscrapers. Although this is just another Manhattan business district and the buildings individually aren't of great note, taken together they form an urban environment of considerable grandeur.

On the right side of Sixth Avenue, north of 50th Street, stands:

7. **Radio City Music Hall,** which has been restored to its 1930s art deco elegance. Its original owner, Samuel "Roxy" Rothafel, ran it as a vaudeville house, but the enterprise was a flop and Rothafel sold out to the Rockefellers. Today shows

Midtown

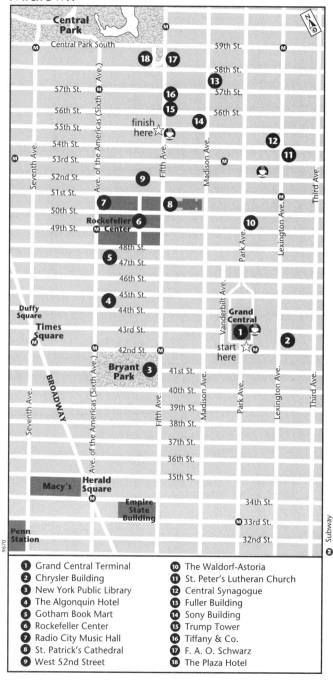

1. Grand Central Terminal
2. Chrysler Building
3. New York Public Library
4. The Algonquin Hotel
5. Gotham Book Mart
6. Rockefeller Center
7. Radio City Music Hall
8. St. Patrick's Cathedral
9. West 52nd Street
10. The Waldorf-Astoria
11. St. Peter's Lutheran Church
12. Central Synagogue
13. Fuller Building
14. Sony Building
15. Trump Tower
16. Tiffany & Co.
17. F. A. O. Schwarz
18. The Plaza Hotel

here run the gamut from performances by headliners such as Liza Minelli to the annual Christmas Spectacular—starring Radio City's own Rockettes and a cast that includes live animals (just try to picture the camels sauntering in through the Sixth Avenue entrance!). Guided tours are available; call 247-4777 for information.

Now take 50th Street east, and cross Fifth Avenue. Between 50th and 51st Streets is:

8. **St. Patrick's Cathedral,** the seat of the Archdiocese of New York. Designed by James Renwick and modeled after Cologne's cathedral, it's a magnificent Gothic-style structure, with twin spires rising 330 feet above street level. Construction took 21 years. Zelda and F. Scott Fitzgerald were married here in 1920, and honeymooned at the nearby Biltmore Hotel (which has since been demolished)—that is, until they proved a bit too rowdy for the management's taste and were asked to leave.

In 1968, funeral services were held in St. Patrick's for slain presidential candidate Bobby Kennedy, then New York's senator. Millions of viewers remained transfixed in front of their TV sets as Ethel, Jackie, and Teddy Kennedy bade him farewell; national figures, including Richard Nixon and Billy Graham, sat in attendance. Mourners lined up for almost a mile outside the great bronze doors of St. Patrick's to pay their respects before Kennedy's body was taken by train to Arlington National Cemetery, where he was interred near his brother John.

Continue uptown on Fifth Avenue toward 52nd Street. Take a look to your left, where:

9. **West 52nd Street** has been designated "Swing Street." You'd never know it just by looking, but this block holds a special place in jazz history. It was lined with a number of illicit speakeasies during Prohibition, and after its repeal, many of the establishments became jazz clubs, nurturing such great talents as Billie Holliday, Fats Waller, Dizzy Gillespie, Charlie Parker, and Sarah Vaughan.

The **Twenty-one Club,** at 21 West 52nd Street, is still a popular restaurant and one of the few establishments to survive from this era. Operating as a speakeasy during Prohibition, it relied on several clever devices to guard against police raids, such as a trap door on the bar that sent everyone's cocktails tumbling into the sewer when a button was pressed.

Now head in the opposite direction (east) on 52nd Street, past Madison Avenue. Cross Park Avenue and make a right so you're heading down the east side of the avenue. As you look down Park, you'll see the old New York Central headquarters (now the Helmsley Building) in a lovely structure that sat astride the avenue crowned with an elaborate cupola without obstructing the view of lower Park Avenue. The building has been totally overshadowed, and the view downtown destroyed by the unimaginative 59-story Met Life building that now towers between the Helmsley Building and Grand Central Terminal. It is, to my mind, New York's greatest architectural travesty.

Continue down Park Avenue past **St. Bartholomew's,** a domed Episcopal church sporting a Byzantine style that seems startling in this location. At 50th Street stands one of the most famous hotels in the world:

10. **The Waldorf-Astoria.** For almost a century, the Waldorf has been synonymous with wealth and luxury. In 1897, in the midst of a devastating economic depression, a society matron, Mrs. Bradley Martin, decided to hold a costume ball at the hotel for 1,200 guests, who were to attend dressed in the style of the court of Versailles. When details of the costly preparations, rumored to top a quarter of a million dollars, hit the papers, outrage ran high. A huge squad of police officers, personally supervised by Police Commissioner Teddy Roosevelt (whose wife was inside enjoying the festivities), had to be positioned around the hotel to prevent the great unwashed from venting their resentment.

Cole Porter and his wife lived here for many years in one of the permanent apartments in the Waldorf Towers; one of the hotel's dining spots, Peacock Alley, still boasts his piano. Other famous residents of these luxury suites have included Gen. Douglas MacArthur, Herbert Hoover, Henry and Clare Booth Luce, and the Duke and Duchess of Windsor. Gangster Lucky Luciano also lived here under an alias until he was forced to leave the Waldorf for less luxurious digs—in the state penitentiary.

Take 50th Street east to Lexington Avenue and turn left, heading north to 53rd Street.

Take a Break   Take 53rd Street west of Lexington Avenue to **Citicorp Center** and enter under the red awning on 53rd Street that says "The Market." (As you walk toward it, you'll get a quick glimpse of the "Lipstick Building" on Lexington Avenue.) If you head downstairs to the plaza level, you'll find café tables scattered under the atrium for those who want to grab a frozen yogurt, a salad, or a sandwich.

More formal dining options here include **La Brochette** for French fare, **Alfredo** for Italian cuisine, and my favorite spot, **Avgerinos,** a Greek café whose sparkling white walls are decorated with brightly colored pottery. Main courses, which run under $15, include chicken souvlaki, roast leg of lamb, moussaka, and stuffed grape leaves, and there's baklava for dessert.

At the southeast corner of 54th Street and Lexington Avenue stands:

11. **St. Peter's Lutheran Church,** a modern structure built in 1977 and adorned with sculpture by Louise Nevelson. St. Peter's is famous for its Sunday evening Jazz Vespers, where many of the greatest names in jazz have performed. Look through the window facing Lexington Avenue to get a glimpse of the striking, almost stark interior.

Just north of St. Peter's, at 55th Street and across Lexington, is the:

12. **Central Synagogue,** one of New York's finest examples of Moorish-Revival–style architecture. The oldest synagogue in continuous use in the city, it was dedicated in 1870.

Just a couple of blocks uptown, you'll turn left onto 57th Street. At the northwest corner of 57th and Lexington is 135 East 57th Street, one of my favorite New York buildings, with a spectacular curved facade.

Fifty-seventh Street is home to many of the city's established art galleries and upscale boutiques. Heading west, you'll come to the beautiful black-and-white art deco:

13. **Fuller Building** at the northeast corner of Madison Avenue and 57th Street. Look at the bronze doors, the marble fixtures, and mosaic floors—and plan to spend some time browsing in the many galleries housed here.

Turn left and head down Madison Avenue. At the southwest corner of Madison and 56th Street stands the:

14. **Sony Building.** Opened in 1983, this pink granite building was formerly the AT&T Building. Once a disciple of Mies van der Rohe, architect Philip Johnson, like his mentor, was known for designing black boxes—stark towers with little or no ornamentation—but he renounced his earlier theories and began to move toward postmodernism, incorporating decorative touches into his designs, such as the distinctive top on this building, which resembles a notched piece of Chippendale furniture.

Walk west on 56th Street toward Fifth Avenue. At the corner, stop to look back at the Sony Building; now you'll get a good view of the top of the tower. Turn right onto Fifth Avenue. Halfway up the block is:

15. **Trump Tower.** This glittery mixed-use cooperative, developed by The Donald himself, has commercial tenants on the lower floors and million-dollar-plus apartments upstairs. (This is where Michael Jackson and Lisa-Marie Presley reportedly holed up after their honeymoon.) Push the huge gold Ts mounted on the doors and you'll enter a posh shopping atrium with a showy 80-foot waterfall and more pink marble than you would have supposed existed in all of Italy.

After a few exhilarating breaths of Mr. Trump's world, exit and continue up Fifth Avenue to:

16. **Tiffany & Co.,** with its windows full of amazing gems. Who could forget Audrey Hepburn as Holly Golightly, gracefully strolling by these same windows in *Breakfast at Tiffany's*? Go in and peruse the display cases; you'll probably see a few customers here choosing engagement rings.

Head uptown on Fifth Avenue, pausing to take a peek at the wildly creative design inside the Warner Brothers store (note the whimsical frieze around the building depicting the many "genres" of cartoons). Just north of 58th Street is the toy store of every child's dreams:

17. **F. A. O. Schwarz.** You may remember Tom Hanks's famous dance interpretation of "Chopsticks," performed here on a giant piano keyboard in the movie *Big*. The stuffed animal department on the first floor is my favorite section;

it's a jungle full of cuddly lions, tigers, and bears. Allow plenty of time to browse through this wonderland of toys.

Across from F. A. O. Schwarz stands the landmark:

18. **Plaza Hotel,** built in 1907. (Back then, suites rented for $25 a night!) Zelda Fitzgerald turned heads here by making a splash (literally) in the fountain in front of the hotel. The Fitzgeralds stayed here in September 1922 while looking for a home, and Scott used the Plaza as the backdrop for a crucial scene in his masterpiece, *The Great Gatsby.* Another famous guest, Frank Lloyd Wright, stayed in a suite overlooking the park while he designed the Guggenheim Museum. Young visitors will be familiar with the Plaza as the heroine's home in the children's classic *Eloise.* And more recently, Eddie Murphy was married here; his guest list ran the gamut from rapper Heavy D. to Tom Jones—and 1,000 of his closest friends.

Head back downtown on Fifth Avenue.

Winding Down There's no better place to stop for an afternoon cocktail than the bar where the Bloody Mary was invented—the **King Cole Bar and Lounge,** in the St. Regis Hotel, 2 East 55th Street, adorned with a wonderful mural of the old monarch himself. There's also an elegant afternoon tea served in the Astor Court, a plush venue with a vaulted ceiling, trompe-l'oeil cloud murals, and exquisite 22-karat gold leafing.

The hotel itself is a landmark, built in 1904 by John Jacob Astor and housing some of the most expensive rooms in the city. Ernest Hemingway, Alfred Hitchcock, and Salvador Dalí all stayed at the St. Regis, and John Lennon and Yoko Ono occupied suites here in the early 1970s.

CENTRAL PARK

Start: Grand Army Plaza, at 59th Street and Fifth Avenue.

Subway: Take the N or R to Fifth Avenue.

Finish: The Vanderbilt Gate, the entrance to the Conservatory Garden, at 105th Street and Fifth Avenue.

Time: Approximately 5 hours, including lunch. If you want to explore more fully (stopping to visit the zoo for an hour or two, for instance), consider breaking up this tour into a two-day excursion.

Best Time: Weekends, weather permitting, when the park hums with activity.

Central Park was designed by landscape architects par excellence Frederick Law Olmsted and Calvert Vaux in the late 1850s, when its land was still on the outskirts of the city. Its advent ensured that New Yorkers would always have recourse to pastoral tranquillity. One of the world's most beautiful urban parks, it's a recreational greenbelt of woodlands, wisteria-shaded arbors, duck- and swan-filled lakes and lagoons, meadows, rambling lanes, gardens, fountains, pavilions, and picturesque bridges. Encompassing 843 acres enclosed by stone walls, the park is $2\frac{1}{2}$ miles long (extending from 59th to 110th Streets) and a half mile wide (from Fifth Avenue to

Central Park West). It is the scene of numerous concerts, theatrical productions, and events ranging from jogging marathons to birdwatching walks. There are playing fields for various sports, bridal trails, biking paths, boating lakes, a lovely zoo, gardens, and playgrounds. One could take an art tour of the dozens of statues dotting the park—many of them geared to children. And on weekends especially, musicians, acrobats, puppeteers, and other enterprising performers offer a wealth of free entertainment. Thanks to the combined efforts of the Central Park Conservancy, which, in concert with the N.Y.C. Parks Department, has spearheaded the renovation of over a third of Central Park over the last decade, the park today is safe, clean, and beautiful.

• • • • • • • • • • • • • • • •

Starting Out   Consider starting out early (about 9am) with a leisurely breakfast at one of the plush luxury hotels near our entrance point—the **Plaza's Palm Court** or **Edwardian Room,** the **Café Pierre at the Pierre,** or the **Fantino Restaurant at the Ritz-Carlton.** All charge about $15, including tax and tip, for a continental breakfast, $25 for a full American breakfast. Much less pricey, but still very nice, is the **Zoo Café,** which offers terrace seating under a wisteria arbor; it's open, as is the zoo, from 10am weekdays, from 10:30am weekends and holidays.

Start at the southeastern corner of the park at:

1. **Grand Army Plaza.** The 59th Street entrance to the park is heralded by Augustus Saint-Gaudens' equestrian statue—today rather garishly regilded—of General William T. Sherman, fronted by an allegorical figure of winged victory. Its unveiling took place on Memorial Day, 1903, with bands playing *Marching Through Georgia* and a military parade (some of Sherman's men were among the marchers). Also at this corner are horse-drawn carriages. Before you enter the park, note the Strand Bookstore's Paris-like kiosks on Fifth Avenue between 60th and 61st Streets. Stop to browse if you like, and consider purchasing their first-rate full-color map of Central Park. It will be helpful on your tour and a nice souvenir of the day.

Cross 60th Street and take the closest path to Fifth Avenue into the park. It leads to the:

2. **Central Park Wildlife Conservation Center (The Central Park Zoo).** In spite of opposition by both Olmsted and Vaux—who feared losing natural scenery to gaudy attractions—there has been some sort of zoo in the park since 1864. No other American city had a zoo in the mid–19th century, and the concept was viewed as a cultural coup for New York by its founders. Originally just a diverse collection of donated animals (Olmsted mockingly opined that they were mostly "pets of children who had died"), early zoo denizens included three African Cape buffaloes acquired by General Sherman during his Georgia siege and circus animals quartered at the zoo in winter by P. T. Barnum. Eight monkeys (purchased rather than donated) were described in *The New York Times* in July 1871, as "comical 'Darwinian links'" (monkeys were of special interest in those still-early days of Darwinian theory). The zoo became a more formal establishment in 1934 when a quadrangle of red- brick animal houses was constructed.

In 1988, a renovated 5.5-acre zoo opened its doors, substituting natural-habitat enclosures for confining cages and exhibiting a cross-section of international wildlife that comprises about 450 animals. Three major ecological areas are arranged around a formal English-style Central Garden that centers on a sea lion pool. The dense jungle-like Tropic Zone, a rain-forest environment with streams and waterfalls, houses an aviary of brightly hued birds, along with monkeys, alligators, reptiles, and amphibians. In the Temperate Territory, Japanese snow monkeys live on an island in a lake inhabited by Arctic whooper swans; this area also has an outdoor pavilion for viewing red pandas. And the Polar Circle is home to penguins, polar bears, harbor seals, and Arctic foxes. Glass-roofed colonnaded walkways shelter zoo visitors from the elements. If you do go in, make sure to see the Intelligence Garden, with wrought-iron chairs under a rustic wooden vine-covered pagoda; it's the perfect spot for quiet contemplation. The zoo is open 365 days a year. Admission is charged.

On the Fifth Avenue side of the zoo is:

3. **The Arsenal,** a fortresslike Gothic Revival building complete with octagonal turrets. Built in the late 1840s (predating the park), it housed troops during the Civil

Central Park

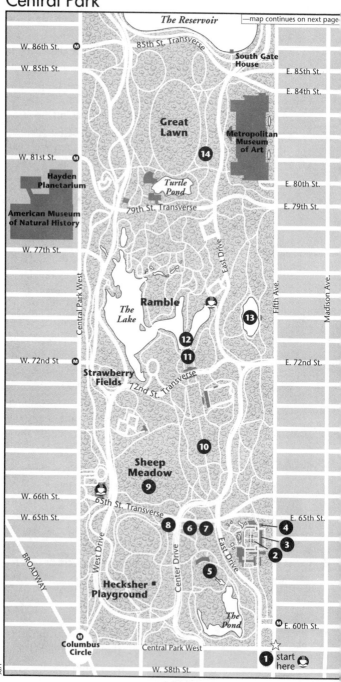

map continues on next page

The Reservoir

85th St. Transverse

W. 86th St.

W. 85th St.

South Gate House

E. 85th St.

E. 84th St.

Great Lawn

Metropolitan Museum of Art

W. 81st St.

Hayden Planetarium

Turtle Pond

E. 80th St.

E. 79th St.

79th St. Transverse

American Museum of Natural History

W. 77th St.

East Drive

Ramble

The Lake

Central Park West

Fifth Ave.

Madison Ave.

13

12

11

W. 72nd St

E. 72nd St.

Strawberry Fields

72nd St. Transverse

10

Sheep Meadow

9

W. 66th St.

West Drive

65th St. Transverse

W. 65th St.

E. 65th St.

8   **6** **7**

4

3

2

5

Heckscher Playground

Center Drive

East Drive

The Pond

Columbus Circle

E. 60th St.

Central Park West

1 start here

W. 58th St.

BROADWAY

9671

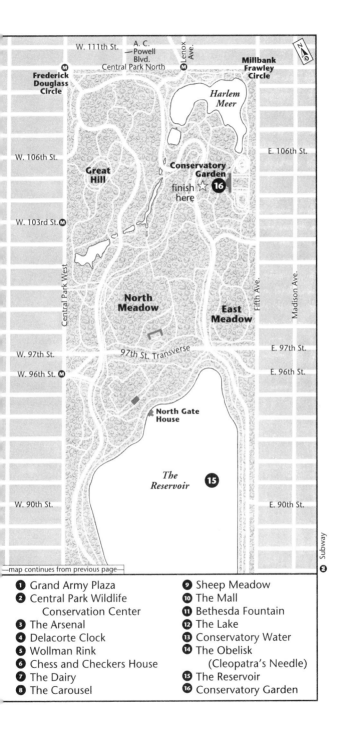

W. 111th St.

A. C. Powell Blvd.

Central Park North

Lenox Ave.

Millbank Frawley Circle

Frederick Douglass Circle

Harlem Meer

W. 106th St.

E. 106th St.

Great Hill

Conservatory Garden

finish here ☆ **16**

W. 103rd St.

North Meadow

East Meadow

Central Park West

Fifth Ave.

Madison Ave.

97th St. Transverse

W. 97th St.

E. 97th St.

W. 96th St.

E. 96th St.

North Gate House

The Reservoir **15**

W. 90th St.

E. 90th St.

Subway

—map continues from previous page—

N

❶ Grand Army Plaza	❾ Sheep Meadow
❷ Central Park Wildlife Conservation Center	❿ The Mall
	⓫ Bethesda Fountain
❸ The Arsenal	⓬ The Lake
❹ Delacorte Clock	⓭ Conservatory Water
❺ Wollman Rink	⓮ The Obelisk (Cleopatra's Needle)
❻ Chess and Checkers House	
❼ The Dairy	⓯ The Reservoir
❽ The Carousel	⓰ Conservatory Garden

War and was the first home of the American Museum of Natural History from 1869 to 1877. Originally, its exterior brick was covered with stucco that was later removed. Today, the brick is ivied and the Arsenal houses park headquarters, zoo administration offices, and a third-floor art gallery. Walk around to the front entrance and note the stair railing made of rifles and the weapon-related embellishments on the facade. Inside, the 1935 WPA mural by Allen Saalburg—depicting maps of New York parks, idyllic 19th-century Central Park scenes, and military themes—merits a look if you're here on a weekday when the building is open.

Up ahead is the:

4. **Delacorte Clock.** Atop an arched brick gate, this whimsical animated clock designed by Andrea Spadini has been enchanting park visitors since the mid-1960s. It features six dancing animals—a tambourine-playing bear, a kangaroo on horn, a hippo violinist, a Panlike pipe-playing goat, a penguin drummer, and an elephant squeezing an accordion. On the hour and half hour, the entire animal assemblage rotates to nursery rhyme tunes, and two bronze monkeys atop the clock strike a bell. "Performances" on the hour are longer. Personally, I never tire of watching the Delacorte Clock.

To get to the next stop, you'll have to double back and make the first right after the Zoo Café, where a sign indicates the way to Wollman Rink. Bear left, cross East Drive, and turn down the first sloped path you come to. Cross Gapstow Bridge on your way to:

5. **Wollman Rink.** This popular skating rink, built into the northern bay of the Pond in 1951, provides skatable ice throughout the winter season. The rest of the year it's drained and used for roller-skating and in-line skating. The rink's refrigerating system broke down in 1980 and remained out of operation until real estate magnate Donald Trump came to the rescue in 1986, bringing in his own construction specialists.

En route to Wollman Rink, you'll traverse the **Pond,** originally the site of DeVoor's Mill Stream. On your left is a fenced-in bird refuge, the **Hallett Nature Sanctuary.**

Where the sanctuary fence ends make a right and walk north around the rink. Make the first right after the end of the rink, then the first left (an uphill slope) to the:

6. **Chess and Checkers House.** A gift from Bernard Baruch in 1952, this octagonal hilltop facility has 10 tables indoors and 24 outside for playing these games, the latter under a rustic wooden arbor covered with vines.

Just ahead (east) is:

7. **The Dairy.** This Gothic Revival storybook stone cottage, designed by Vaux in 1870, was originally intended to serve fresh milk and snacks to children. Cows were stabled in a nearby building. Today, the Dairy serves as an information center and houses exhibits on the design and history of the park. You can pick up an events calendar and informative brochures here and check out video information terminals. The Dairy also provides chess and checker games for use at the above-mentioned facility.

Double back, going west past the Chess and Checkers House (take the path on your right), and go through the tunnel (Playmates Arch) under Center Drive to:

8. **The Carousel.** This charming Victorian merry-go-round—originally turned by a blind mule and a horse—is one of the oldest concessions in the park. Its calliope has been playing old-fashioned tunes since 1872. The colorful whirling steeds are among the largest carousel horses in the world. Go ahead; take a ride.

Continuing west (take the path left of the carousel), you'll be walking past the Heckscher ballfields. When you come to West Drive, go north a short way (Tavern on the Green is across the street).

Take a Break **Tavern on the Green** is located in the park at West 67th Street (tel. 873-3200). Its Victorian building was erected in 1870 to house the 200 sheep that grazed on the Sheep Meadow (see Stop 9, below). The dazzling dining room, which Mayor Fiorello LaGuardia opened with a brass key, dates to 1934. In 1976, Hollywood mogul Werner LeRoy renovated Tavern on the Green to the tune of $20 million, creating an unparalleled setting for celebrity-studded parties, film premières, and political functions. It offers patio seating under the trees in a magnificent flower garden (40,000 bulbs—daffodils, tulips, hyacinth—blossom every spring, followed by wisteria and azalea, lilac trees, a riot of chrysanthemums in fall, and winter blooms such as holly and forsythia). There's also indoor dining, with verdant park views, in the lavish glass-enclosed Crystal Room. But the food here is not the point; you go to enjoy the sylvan setting. Lunch and brunch menus include homemade pasta dishes and an array of other items ranging from Dover sole meunière to a chicken club sandwich on toasted brioche. Entrées at either meal average $20; weekdays there's also a three-course prix-fixe lunch for $15 to $25, depending on your entrée. Open for lunch Monday through Friday from 11:30am to 3:45pm, for brunch Saturdays and Sundays from 10am to 3:30pm. Reservations are suggested. Off-hours you can enjoy cocktails in the garden or the lounge.

Make a right on the first path you come to after Tavern on the Green as you make your way north on West Drive (a statue of 19th-century Italian revolutionary Giuseppe Mazzini is directly across the street). The path borders the:

9. **Sheep Meadow.** Originally mandated as a military parade ground, about which Olmsted was less than enthusiastic, the Sheep Meadow took on a more peaceful incarnation in 1878. From that year, until 1934, a flock of Southdown sheep grazed here, tended by a shepherd. Though undoubtedly picturesque, the sheep became deformed from inbreeding over the years and were banished (though only to Prospect Park in Brooklyn) by Parks Commissioner Robert Moses; the shepherd was reassigned to the lion house in the zoo. During the 1960s, the Sheep Meadow was a hippie haven—the setting for antiwar protests, Love-Ins, Be-Ins, and, after the 1969 Stonewall riots that launched the gay pride movement, a Gay-In. Today the lush green Sheep Meadow is a popular spot for kite flyers, sunbathers, picnickers, and frisbee players—a tranquil oasis where loud radios are off limits.

Follow the fence on your right, and make a right where it turns onto the gravel path of the Lilac Walk. After you pass the volleyball court area, cross the road and look for the bronze *Indian Hunter* statue by 19th-century American artist John Quincy Adams Ward. Straight ahead (look for a group of statues) is:

10. **The Mall.** Designed as a Versailles-like grand promenade, this shaded formal walkway, about a quarter of a mile in length, is bordered by a double row of stately American elms that form a cathedral arch overhead. At its entrance are statues of Columbus (created in 1892 to mark the 400th anniversary of his voyage), Shakespeare (like the *Indian Hunter*, by J. Q. A. Ward; Shakespearean actor Edwin Booth laid its cornerstone), Robert Burns, Sir Walter Scott, and American poet Fitz-Greene Halleck.

Make the first right at the end of the Mall and continue north around the back of the bandshell through the Wisteria Pergola. At the opposite end of the Mall, across East 72nd Street, a broad stairway—its massive sandstone balustrade ornately decorated with birds, flowers, and fruit—descends to one of the park's most stunning vistas:

11. **Bethesda Fountain.** Emma Stebbins's biblically inspired neoclassical winged Bethesda (the "angel of the waters") tops a vast triple-tiered stone fountain with the lake forming a scenic backdrop. Its setting is Vaux's part Gothic, part Romanesque terrace, the heart of the park and one of its most popular venues. Like the Sheep Meadow, Bethesda Fountain was a hippie hub in the 1960s filled with counterculture types demonstrating against the Vietnam War, smoking pot, and strumming guitars. A *Newsweek* article of that era dubbed it "Freak Fountain" and called it the "craziest, gayest, gathering place in the city." Today it is no longer a scene, but it remains one of New York's most idyllic settings.

Go down the steps (taking time to look closely at the bas-reliefs on the balustrades), and make a right on the path closest to:

12. **The Lake.** Its perimeter pathway lined with weeping willows and Japanese cherry trees, the $22^1/_2$-acre lake was created from Sawkill Creek which entered the Park near West 79th Street. The neo-Victorian Loeb Boathouse at the east end of the Lake rents rowboats and bicycles; evenings you can arrange gondola rides. Along the path to the lake, you'll

usually see handwriting analysts, acupressure masseurs, reflexologists, and other purveyors of New Age services.

Take a Break   The **Boathouse Café** (tel. 517-2233), at the eastern end of the Lake, is just heavenly. Open from early spring to late October, it offers al fresco lakeside seating on a wooden deck under a white canvas canopy. Overhead heaters allow for the café's extended season. The menu is contemporary American, featuring nouvelle pasta dishes, salads, focaccia sandwiches, and heartier entrées such as pan-fried yellowfin tuna with ginger crust, served with mango relish and mashed potatoes. Scrumptious fresh-baked breads are a plus, though, as at Tavern on the Green, the setting is much more of a draw than the food. Lunch and brunch entrées average around $16. Lunch hours are Monday through Friday from noon to 4pm and Saturday from 11am to 4pm; Sunday brunch is served from 11am to 4pm. An outdoor bar offers light fare, drinks, and desserts.

The café is very elegant, but if you want something simpler—and less expensive—the Boathouse complex also houses a **cafeteria** with both indoor and outdoor seating. It serves full and continental breakfasts, sandwiches, chili, fresh fruit, and other light-fare items. Open year-round. Hours are 9am to 6:30pm daily in summer, closing a little earlier the rest of the year.

From the south end of the Boathouse, cross East Drive and follow the path to the:

13. **Conservatory Water.** The above-mentioned Pond and Lake are free-form bodies of water. The Conservatory Water, scene of model boat races (there's even a model boathouse on the Fifth Avenue side where miniature craft are stored) is of formal design. Originally planned as the setting for a conservatory garden (built later and located further uptown; see Stop 16), it is the site of José de Creeft's *Alice in Wonderland* statues (Alice, the Mad Hatter, March Hare, Dormouse, and Cheshire Cat) inspired by the John Tenniel illustrations in the original 1865 edition. Overlooking the water is George Lober's Hans Christian Andersen Memorial Statue, complete with Ugly Duckling. This gift from Denmark is the setting for storytelling sessions every Saturday from June through September. Circle the pond,

and peek in the model boathouse if it's open.

Exit the Conservatory Water on the northwest path (past Alice), and continue through Glade Arch, turning left after the 79th Street Tranverse and following the path under Greywacke Arch. Make the first right turn on the other side of the arch to:

14. **The Obelisk (Cleopatra's Needle).** This 3,500-year-old, 77-foot-high, Egyptian pink granite obelisk was a gift to New York City from the khedive of Egypt in 1881— to thank America for its help in building the Suez Canal. William Vanderbilt paid the cost of transportation (over $100,000), a complicated affair that involved the construction of a railroad track from the Hudson River. The obelisk immediately became a major park attraction; gazing upon it, noted the *Herald,* "was regarded as a far greater treat by the majority of park visitors than to watch the wondrous developments of nature." Dating from the reign of King Thutmose III in 1600 B.C., the obelisk stood in front of the Temple of the Sun in Heliopolis, Egypt, until it was removed by the Romans in 12 B.C. and placed at the approach of a temple built by Cleopatra (hence its nickname). Its hieroglyphics (which are translated here, a gift of Cecil B. de Mille) tell of the deeds of Thutmose III, Ramses II, and Osarkon I. The four bronze crabs peeking out from each corner of the base are 19th-century replicas of the originals, which—it is believed—were placed there by the Romans as a decorative means of support. Crabs were objects of worship to the ancient Egyptians.

Follow the path behind (west of) the obelisk. When it ends, bear right and follow East Drive, keeping to the left. Soon you'll come to steps and a cast-iron bridge leading to the South Gate House. Make a right onto the jogging path of the:

15. **Reservoir,** created in 1862 to supply New York City's water system. Occupying 106 acres and extending the width of the park, it is girded by bridle and jogging paths. The Reservoir holds a billion gallons of water when full, is 40 feet at its greatest depth, and supplies about 10% of the city's water; the path around it is 1.57 miles long. Walk—or jog— along the eastern border of the Reservoir, getting off at 96th

Street (a playground is diagonally across). At press time, there was a movement to rename the Reservoir in honor of Jacqueline Kennedy Onassis, who loved Central Park.

Continue north on East Drive to 102nd Street, exit the park, and walk north along Fifth Avenue to the Vanderbilt Gate. This ornate portal, designed in Paris in 1894, formerly heralded the Fifth Avenue mansion of Cornelius Vanderbilt II. Fittingly adorned with plant motifs, it is the entrance to the:

16. **Conservatory Garden.** This formal garden—its symmetrical paths and arbor walks contrasting with the natural look of the rest of the park—was originally the site of a complex of glass greenhouses built in 1899. They were dismantled in 1934, when Parks Commissioner Robert Moses deemed maintenance costs too high. He commissioned the current garden as a WPA project in 1936. As you enter from Fifth Avenue, you'll be facing the elegant Italian garden—a greensward with no flower beds centering on a classic fountain. It is ringed with yew hedges and bordered by allées of crabapple trees. In spring the crabapples bloom with pink and white flowers and narcissus grows in the ivy beneath them.

Walk through the allée on the left to the lovely mazelike English garden. It contains the bronze statue of the children from *The Secret Garden* standing in a reflecting pool. In summer there are water lilies and a wide variety of flowering plants and shrubs—roses, butterfly bush, day lilies, clusters of blue forget-me-nots, geraniums, foxglove, and many more. Now walk through the Wisteria Pergola (at the back of the Italian garden). This flower-bedecked wrought-iron arbor, especially magnificent in late May, connects the English and French gardens.

In the French garden, entered via rose-covered arched trellises, two levels of exquisite flower beds encircle the Untermeyer Fountain that centers on an enchanting sculpture of dancing maidens (my favorite in the park) by Walter Schott. Here 20,000 tulips bloom in spring and 5,000 chrysanthemums in fall.

THE UPPER WEST SIDE

Start: 86th Street and Broadway.

Subway: Take the 1 or 9 to 86th Street.

Finish: Lincoln Center.

Time: 3¹/₂ hours (allow more time for shopping, refreshment stops, and museum visits)

Best Time: Weekday afternoons, when shops and museums are open but crowds are at a minimum.

The Upper West Side has undergone a decidedly upwardly mobile transformation in the last few decades. Though some magnificent luxury apartment buildings have stood here since the days of gaslights and horse-drawn carriages, for the first half of the 20th century they were surrounded by an otherwise unremarkable, largely working-class neighborhood. Then came Lincoln Center.

A massive urban renewal effort centered around the construction of this performing arts complex in the early 1960s. Blocks of dilapidated housing and bodegas gave way to pricey boutiques and exclusive residential buildings.

Gentrification almost completely swallowed up the West Side in the decades that followed, but dozens of mom-and-pop dry cleaners and shoe repair shops still remain, giving the West Side its unique flavor. Especially as you go further uptown, you might spot a neighborhood barber shop still going strong even though a trendy new hair salon has opened nearby, or you'll suddenly come upon a block where the signs are in Spanish and the sounds of salsa blast from everyone's windows.

Some old-timers bemoan the changes, but after the yuppie invasion of the 1970s and 1980s, the West Side has maintained a more democratic and informal atmosphere than the staid and stuffy East Side. This neighborhood pulses with life. It is, for the most part, a literate, educated, and liberal community, full of young families—people speak of stroller gridlock on the sidewalks. Joggers, dog owners, and basketball players take advantage of the proximity to both Central and Riverside Parks. Residents pride themselves on the wonderful food shopping at Fairway and Zabar's; they can enjoy an authentic Cuban dinner in a simple little hole in the wall one night and dine in an elegant French bistro or a sleek sushi bar the next.

The tour that follows will introduce you to the highlights of the West Side: the great shopping along Broadway and Columbus Avenue, the architectural masterpieces along Central Park West, and Lincoln Center, the heart of New York's cultural life.

• • • • • • • • • • • • • • • •

From the 86th Street subway station, walk south down the east side of Broadway to 84th Street ("Edgar Allan Poe Street"). Just off Broadway to your left is:

1. **215 West 84th Street.** As recently as the 1840s, this area was still undeveloped rural countryside. Edgar Allan Poe lived briefly with his wife in a farmhouse that stood here on a rocky knoll. He completed *The Raven* in the summer of 1844. A plaque (on the other side of Broadway) commemorates his stay.

Go back to Broadway and cross the street; turn left, heading downtown. Between 83rd and 82nd Streets, you'll pass the:

2. **Barnes & Noble** superstore, which has caused quite an uproar on the West Side. When the store first opened a couple of years ago, residents felt that suburbia was creeping into their neighborhood, and worried that their favorite neighborhood and specialty bookstores would not survive the competition. Many devotees of nearby

Shakespeare & Co. (see below) swore never to set foot in Barnes & Noble—but soon the store was an undeniable hit. Offering substantial discounts on all its best-selling titles, Barnes & Noble has won over the neighborhood with a café that features Starbucks coffee and lots of comfortable desks and chairs for hours of uninterrupted browsing. *Note:* On Saturday nights, the store turns into quite a pickup scene for single young West Siders.

Just a block downtown, at the corner of 81st Street, **Shakespeare & Co.** is still going strong despite the presence of the new superstore. Always a favorite among the neighborhood's rumpled intellectuals, it's known for carefully chosen selections (including many offerings from small presses), personal service, and extremely knowledgeable staff.

At the northwest corner of 80th Street and Broadway stands:

3. **Zabar's,** another West Side retail institution. The faint of heart should beware: Zabar's is sheer bedlam, and its crowd of serious shoppers will shove you right out of the way for the perfect wheel of Brie. But plunge into the crowds and wander through the aisles for a truly mind-boggling selection of imported cheeses, breads, cold cuts, salads, and appetizers. The aroma of freshly ground coffee pervades the store. At the fish counter you can get anything from smoked salmon to caviar. If you're taking this tour on a beautiful spring day, you'll find the fixings here for a memorable picnic feast in Central Park (coming up later on the tour).

Don't be daunted either by the long lines you are sure to see emanating from **H & H Bagels,** just across 80th Street. As anyone in the neighborhood will tell you, these are the best bagels in town—so fresh they're still warm from the oven. Gothamites who have moved away from New York still beg their friends to Fed-Ex H & H bagels to them.

Just south rises the magnificent limestone facade of:

4. **The Apthorp,** which commands an entire square block bounded by 78th and 79th Streets, Broadway, and West End Avenue. Admire the building from the Broadway side, standing in front of the stately iron gates that lead into a landscaped central courtyard with a pair of fountains, marble benches, and statuary.

Turn right and take 78th Street west, heading away from the bustle of Broadway. Then turn left down West End Avenue. At the northeast corner of 77th Street stands the Flemish-style:

5. **West End Collegiate Church and School,** with dormer windows and a steep red-tiled roof. The church was completed in 1892 for the Collegiate Reformed Protestant Dutch Church, a congregation formed by Dutch colonists in 1628. The Collegiate School, established by the church in 1638, is one of the oldest independent secondary schools in the country.

Proceed east on 77th Street back to Broadway and head downtown. At 74th Street, you'll pass **Fairway,** West Siders' favorite produce store. Even in winter, fresh fruits and vegetables abound here, as do radicchio-seeking shoppers who prowl the store's aisles at just about any hour of the day. A block further south, you'll see the splendid Beaux Arts–style:

6. **Ansonia Hotel,** between 73rd and 74th Streets, built as a luxury residential hotel and completed in 1904. Its architect, W. E. D. Stokes, bought this parcel of land, then surrounded by single-family homes, and decided to raise eyebrows by building a 17-story "tenement" in flamboyant French style. Resembling a lacy, opulent wedding cake, the Ansonia sports a three-story mansard roof and rounded corner towers capped with high domes.

Luxurious apartment houses were all the rage at the turn of the century, and the Ansonia's early tenants were lured by an incredible series of amenities and services. Messages propelled pneumatically in a network of tubes could be sent from room to room. There was a grand ballroom, a swimming pool, a trellised roof garden, a theater, a barber shop, a pharmacist, a florist, and a laundry. And live seals splashed about in the lobby's fountain! There were several restaurants where tenants could dine or have meals sent up to their suites. Stokes himself kept a small pet bear, goats, and chickens in the roof garden; he sold the eggs to tenants at a discount.

The Ansonia has always been a favorite address for musicians, among them Stravinsky, Toscanini, and Caruso. (The apartments here are virtually soundproof, so musicians can

The Upper West Side

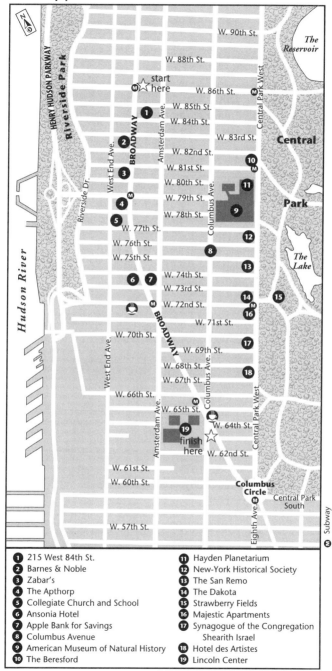

1. 215 West 84th St.
2. Barnes & Noble
3. Zabar's
4. The Apthorp
5. Collegiate Church and School
6. Ansonia Hotel
7. Apple Bank for Savings
8. Columbus Avenue
9. American Museum of Natural History
10. The Beresford
11. Hayden Planetarium
12. New-York Historical Society
13. The San Remo
14. The Dakota
15. Strawberry Fields
16. Majestic Apartments
17. Synagogue of the Congregation Shearith Israel
18. Hotel des Artistes
19. Lincoln Center

practice without fear of disturbing other tenants.) Other famous residents over the years have included Florenz Ziegfeld and actress Billie Burke.

The golden age of the Ansonia ended with the Great Depression, and the building has seen decades of decline marked by repeated legal battles between tenants and owners. It was, however, declared a landmark in 1972. (You may recognize it as the setting for the recent movie *Single White Female.*)

Just downtown from the Ansonia is **HMV,** a music store with three floors of CDs, tapes, and videos—everything from Louis Armstrong to ZZ Top. There's a remarkable selection of world beat, jazz, dance, and progressive music; a large section devoted to Broadway and film scores; and headsets that let you sample some of the new releases before buying. There's also a well-stocked classical music annex around the corner on 72nd Street.

Take a Break   Tucked away in a basement on the downtown side of 72nd Street between Broadway and West End Avenue is a real find, a pub that hosts a crowd of

The Ghosts of Baseball Legends

A significant bit of baseball history transpired in the Ansonia. Members of the Chicago White Sox plotted to fix the World Series during a stay here in 1919. The ringleader, Chick Gandil, first approached pitcher Lefty Williams on the street in front of the building. Later the conspirators met upstairs to plan their strategy; Eddie Cicotte returned to his room to find $10,000 under his pillow. Ironically, Babe Ruth, who almost singlehandedly restored fans' faith in baseball after that disastrous scandal, moved into an 11-room suite in the same building when he donned the New York Yankees' uniform in 1920. Ruth's years in the Ansonia were the height of his blustering, carousing career, marked by eating too much, drinking too much, womanizing, and staying out all night. But the press barely covered his scandalous exploits; New Yorkers loved him too much.

neighborhood regulars. The **All State Cafe,** 250 West 72nd Street (tel. 874-1883), serves typical bar food—fried calamari, spicy chicken wings, and bowls of chili—plus surprisingly good daily specials. The thick, juicy burgers are among the best in town. Peter, the bartender, makes a mean margarita, and offers an impressive selection of whiskies. If you're there on a chilly winter day, you'll appreciate the fire crackling in the hearth beside the bar. And there's a great selection of classic rock, jazz, oldies, and swing tunes on the jukebox. The All State is open daily from 11:30am to 1am (later on weekends).

Go back to Broadway and 73rd Street; now take 73rd Street east across Broadway. Between 73rd and 74th Streets is the:

7. **Apple Bank for Savings,** designed by York & Sawyer in the 1920s and boasting a massive limestone facade and stunning ironwork doors. The structure's unique trapezoid shape allows it to fill out the plot of land created where Broadway cuts diagonally across Amsterdam Avenue. And its heavy, monumental style is perfectly suited to a bank building. You'll pass beneath a beautiful decorative clock, topped with twin lions.

At 73rd and Amsterdam is **Star Magic,** an exciting space-age emporium filled with telescopes, prisms, models, gemstones, jewelry, New Age CDs, globes, and books—something to satisfy anyone with a sense of adventure and curiosity about the universe.

Continue east on 73rd Street to:

8. **Columbus Avenue,** one of New York's trendiest promenades, lined with boutiques, coffee bars, and restaurants. Stores spring up like weeds on Columbus—and they disappear as fast as yesterday's news. Take this part of the stroll to stop and browse in any place that catches your eye. Exotiqa II (no. 284) offers international crafts (look for the colorful Indonesian cats). Try Sacha of London (no. 294) and Kenneth Cole (no. 353) for up-to-the-minute styles in shoes. There's Oaktree (no. 306) for men's fashions and Vari Zioni (no. 309) and Putumayo (no. 341) for women's.

While you're meandering up Columbus, take a peek off to your left at **150 West 75th Street,** where Anaïs Nin lived with her mother and brother from 1914 to 1919. In the first-floor rooming house at this address, the teenage writer began penning the diary that became her most important work.

Continue your stroll up Columbus, taking your time to allow for optimum people-watching. As you cross 77th Street, you'll see the grounds of the:

9. **American Museum of Natural History.** The famous Hall of Dinosaurs, housing several skeletons of our prehistoric predecessors, has been the hit of many a school field trip over the years. Other highlights include an impressive collection of pre-Columbian artifacts and the largest meteorite ever retrieved. Admission is charged; the museum's hours are Sunday through Thursday from 10am to 5:45pm, and Friday and Saturday from 10am to 8:45pm.

Continue up Columbus to 81st Street; make a right and head toward Central Park West. On your left, crowning the northwest corner of the intersection is:

10. **The Beresford,** the first in a long line of architectural gems you'll pass on Central Park West. The Beresford, with its baroque tower and classical ornamentation, is an adaptation of an Italian Renaissance palazzo. Its architect, Emery Roth, was a Jewish immigrant who arrived in this country flat broke as a teenager. He taught himself design and, through sheer hard work and determination, became one of the city's most noted architects. However, he ran up against shameful anti-Semitism when he applied for membership in the American Institute of Architects and was only admitted after months of lobbying by a fellow architect with better social credentials.

Apartments at the Beresford are hard to come by and run into the millions of dollars. Gangster Meyer Lansky lived here in the 1940s, and more recently, actor Rock Hudson lived here until his death from AIDS in 1985. Other famous residents have included Margaret Mead, who used to walk to work nearby at the Museum of Natural History, plus Beverly Sills, Tony Randall, Mike Nichols, and Helen Gurley Brown.

Make a 180-degree turn and you'll see the:

11. **Hayden Planetarium,** topped by a copper dome. (You may remember that Woody Allen fell in love with Diane Keaton while strolling through a moonscape here in *Manhattan*). There are two floors of exhibitions on the sun, moon, and stars, and your admission includes one of the planetarium's glittering Sky Shows. Admission is charged.

Turn right and head down Central Park West. (Turn back and look up at the Beresford after a half block or so for a better perspective.) Just south of the planetarium is another entrance to the Museum of Natural History, marked by an equestrian statue of Teddy Roosevelt. At the southwest corner of 77th Street and Central Park West you'll see the:

12. **New-York Historical Society,** a rich repository of artifacts, artworks, and documents that chronicle the city's history. In addition to its renowned research library, the museum's highlights include John James Audubon's *Birds of America* watercolor series, a wonderful gallery of Tiffany lamps, and an extensive collection of early American art. The Society has run into funding difficulties in the last few years, so if you want to go inside, call in advance (tel. 873-3400) for current hours of operation.

Once home to heavyweight boxing champ Jack Dempsey and actress and pinup idol Rita Hayworth:

13. **The San Remo,** 145–146 Central Park West, between 74th and 75th Streets, is another grand apartment building bearing the stamp of Emery Roth. The two towers rising at each end are crowned with columned temples. After struggling through the Depression, the owners sold the San Remo and the Beresford together in 1940 for the shocking sum of $25,000 over the combined mortgages.

At Central Park West and 72nd Street is a world-famous architectural masterpiece:

14. **The Dakota,** one of the first luxury apartment buildings in New York. Legend has it that the building's name came about when Edward Clark, the project's developer, was teased by his friends that the site was so far north of the city center that it might as well have been in Dakota territory. Architect Henry J. Hardenbergh, who also designed New

York's landmark Plaza Hotel, created a brooding, Germanic structure accented with gables, dormers, and oriel windows and surrounded by a "dry moat."

(The fortresslike building is so atmospheric, in fact, that it served as the backdrop to the horror movie *Rosemary's Baby.*)

The list of tenants at this prestigious address has included Lauren Bacall, Leonard Bernstein, and Boris Karloff. But the Dakota will forever be associated with its most famous resident, John Lennon, who was gunned down just outside the building.

Lennon was returning to his home in the Dakota after a recording session on December 8, 1980, when he was shot by Mark David Chapman, a lone psychopath who had asked for the former Beatle's autograph only hours earlier. Lennon's widow, Yoko Ono, still lives in the Dakota.

Just inside the 72nd Street entrance to Central Park lies:

15. **Strawberry Fields,** a memorial to Lennon. The three-acre teardrop-shaped "international garden of peace" is adorned with more than 150 species of plants (gifts from as many nations) and 2,500 strawberry plants. Near the entrance, a star-shaped black-and-white tile mosaic—a gift from Naples, Italy—spells out the word "Imagine." Yoko Ono provided the money for the garden's construction and maintenance.

Central Park is also a terrific vantage point from which to see the tops of the buildings you have just passed on Central Park West.

As you exit the park to continue on your route downtown, you'll be right across the street from the:

16. **Majestic Apartments,** another of the grand apartment houses that define the Central Park West skyline. Until the 12-story Hotel Majestic was built in the 1890s, this site was occupied by wooden shacks and grazing goats. It was a sumptuous venue that hosted the likes of Sarah Bernhardt, Edna Ferber, Gustav Mahler, and Vaslav Nijinsky. In 1929, developer Irwin Chanin initiated plans to build a single-tower, 45-story structure. The months that followed, however, saw the stock market crash, so Chanin altered his plans and came up with the 29-story, twin-towered structure you see today between 71st and 72nd Streets. He also broke with tradition by scorning the classical European

models used for most large residential buildings in New York; instead he chose an adaptation of art deco style he called Modern American. The building was ready for tenants in 1931, but the Depression grew so severe that Chanin had defaulted on his mortgage by 1933.

The Majestic is also connected to two major scandals. Bruno Richard Hauptmann, who was prosecuted for kidnapping the Lindbergh baby, was employed as a carpenter here when the crime was committed. And a gangland hit took place in the lobby in 1957, when mobster Frank Costello was shot in the head.

Further down Central Park West, at the southwest corner of 70th Street, you'll see the:

17. Synagogue of the Congregation Shearith Israel,

which dates from 1897. It's home to the oldest Jewish congregation in the United States, which was founded in 1654 by Spanish and Portuguese immigrants who came to New York via Brazil.

Turn right onto 67th Street, where several buildings contain double-height studio apartments. At no. 1 is the Gothic-style:

18. Hotel des Artistes, full of enchanting touches, such as

the row of gargoyles found below the third-floor windows.

Most of the units in the Hotel des Artistes are duplexes and double-height studios. One particularly noteworthy apartment, designed for philanthropist Aaron Naumburg and completed in 1921, has 18-foot ceilings, a wood-balustraded balcony, and lavishly carved woodwork. Naumberg's home was graced with tapestries, fine carpets, antique Italian furniture, paintings, carved figures, and stained-glass windows—and so spectacular was it that all the furnishings and artwork were taken to the Fogg Museum in Cambridge and re-created as an annex after Naumberg's death.

The Hotel des Artistes has attracted an astounding number of famous residents, including Rudolph Valentino, Nöel Coward, Isadora Duncan, Alexander Woollcott, Edna Ferber, former mayor John Lindsay, former governor Hugh Carey, Norman Rockwell, and Emil Fuchs, portraitist to Queen Victoria. (Fuchs, dying of cancer, committed suicide in the

Hotel des Artistes in 1929 by shooting himself with a pearl-handled revolver inscribed by Edward VII.)

The ground floor houses the elegant and romantic **Café des Artistes;** peek in the window to see the restaurant's famous wood-nymph murals by Howard Chandler Christy, a longtime tenant in the building. (Some of the models used for the nymphs have returned to dine in the café over the years.) Christy's murals and his other depictions of lovely ladies in magazine and book illustrations earned him an invitation to be the sole judge at the first Miss America contest.

Continue west on 67th Street to Columbus Avenue and make a left. Between 65th and 66th Streets stands the **Museum of American Folk Art** annex and its gift shop, stocked with books, jewelry, hand-painted pitchers and vases, prints, and one-of-a-kind greeting cards. Across Broadway, you can't miss:

19. **Lincoln Center,** the city's premier venue for the performing arts. In 1956, a committee headed by John D. Rockfeller III selected the site for Lincoln Center, in what was then a rundown residential area. *West Side Story* was filmed in these streets before an astounding 188 buildings were demolished to clear the area; 1,600 people had to be relocated to make way for the project.

The committee commissioned a group of architects headed by Wallace K. Harrison; each building they created has classical lines, and is covered in Italian travertine. The centerpiece of the complex is an outdoor plaza graced with a café terrace and a splashing fountain. New Yorkers enjoy free entertainment under the stars here on the plaza in summer, and in December, one of the city's most beautiful Christmas trees is mounted here.

Left of the plaza is Avery Fisher Hall, with a peristyle of 44 columns soaring seven stories high. It's home to the New York Philharmonic, which has counted among its musical directors such luminaries as Zubin Mehta, Arturo Toscanini, Leopold Stokowski, and Leonard Bernstein. On the right side of the fountain is the New York State Theater, designed by architect Philip Johnson, which hosts performances by the New York City Opera and the New York City Ballet, which was founded by George Balanchine.

Forming the background of the plaza is the Metropolitan Opera House, which boasts a marble colonnade 10 stories high. Inside the glass facade, you can see two large, splendid murals by Marc Chagall. This is the home of the renowned Metropolitan Opera, one of the most prestigious companies in the world for more than a century; acclaimed stars such as Placido Domingo, Luciano Pavarotti, Jose Carreras, Kathleen Battle, and Marilyn Horne have graced the stage here. In early summer, the Opera House also hosts the American Ballet Theatre's season. The Met's interior houses seven rehearsal halls and space to store scenery for as many as 15 operas.

The remainder of the complex at Lincoln Center includes the Guggenheim Bandshell, used for free outdoor concerts; the Vivian Beaumont and Mitzi Newhouse Theaters; the Julliard School, the country's premier academy for the performing arts; and Alice Tully Hall. Also at Lincoln Center is a branch of the New York Public Library, which serves as both a library and a museum of the performing arts. The library hosts an impressive array of free films and concerts.

One-hour tours of Lincoln Center are offered for a small fee; call 875-5350 to check on the day's tour schedule and to make advance reservations. Calendars of upcoming events, including free concerts, are available.

Winding Down Almost any craving can be satisfied at **The Saloon,** 1920 Broadway, at 64th Street (tel. 874-1500), where the specialty is light, creative American and continental fare. The kitchen is rather uneven—the menu is so large that the more ambitious offerings sometimes fail—but the basic salads, burgers, individual pizzas, and sandwiches are all dependably good and prices are moderate. In summer the outdoor café tables offer great people-watching. You'll occasionally see the roller-skating waiters and waitresses dodging tables, diners, and the many passersby who crowd this street.

THE UPPER EAST SIDE

Start: The southeast corner of Central Park, at 59th Street and Fifth Avenue.

Subway: Take the N or R to Fifth Avenue.

Finish: 91st Street and Fifth Avenue.

Time: Approximately 3 hours.

Best Time: Weekday afternoons, when museums and restaurants are open but not as crowded as on Saturdays.

Worst Time: Sundays, when most stores and galleries are closed and the streets seem deserted.

O ver a century ago, society watchers predicted that the wealthy and fashionable would settle permanently on the avenues bordering Central Park. Time has proven them right. Fifth Avenue north of Grand Army Plaza, which lies at the southeast corner of the park, is officially called Museum Mile. But the magnificent private mansions built here in the first few decades of this century by some of America's wealthiest industrial tycoons also earned it the title of Million-aires' Row. Judging from old photos, it was something to behold.

Today, patrician mansions still stand along the avenue, though others have ceded their places to large apartment houses.

But the age of imperial living isn't over by any means. Some of the buildings on Fifth (as well as on Park Avenue and elsewhere on the East Side) contain apartments that are every bit as palatial and sumptuous as the now vanished mansions. Even New Yorkers are surprised to hear of apartments with 20, 30, or even 40 rooms—but they do exist in this neighborhood.

• • • • • • • • • • • • • • • • •

Start your tour on 59th Street, and take a peek over the wall into Central Park. You'll glimpse a pastoral scene—ducks and geese gliding along a pond, and New Yorkers strolling along picturesque walking paths—that contrasts with the urban chaos of the city. You'll explore the park in depth in Tour 8. For now, walk toward Fifth Avenue and the 59th Street entrance to the park, where you'll come upon:

1. **Grand Army Plaza,** adorned with a brilliant gold statue of William Tecumseh Sherman, the ruthless but effective Civil War general who devastated the southern countryside and brought the civilian population to its knees with the Union army's "March to the Sea." "War is cruelty and you cannot refine it," Sherman once observed—but sculptor Augustus Saint-Gaudens has tried, creating a classical equestrian statue of the crusty general and Winged Victory.

A block uptown, between 60th and 61st Streets, contrast this representation of war and its heroes with *The Other Monument,* a 1994 work by Judith Shea, constructed in American folk style and created specifically for this site. This simple depiction of a naked man upon a horse, with real hair used for the rider's head and the horse's tail, stands upon a simple pedestal of rough wooden planks. This striking, subtle work, created a century after the Sherman memorial, speaks of emancipation and the underlying meaning of the Civil War for individual citizens, while the great Saint-Gaudens, working within the traditions of classical sculpture that still influenced 19th-century artists, chose to interpret his subject as a larger-than-life heroic figure.

Now stroll up Fifth Avenue. In good weather you'll see bookstalls from The Strand lining the park, full of used volumes that you can purchase for a fraction of the cover price. On the east (right) side of Fifth Avenue, at 61st

Street, is:

2. **The Pierre,** one of Manhattan's priciest and most exclusive hotels since its opening in 1930. In 1932, mystery writer Dashiell Hammett stayed here while working on *The Thin Man*—though, unfortunately, he couldn't pay the bill he finally ran up. He allegedly donned a disguise to sneak out without settling his tab. If you're starting out early in the morning, breakfast at the Pierre makes for a pricey but elegant beginning to your tour.

At the southeast corner of 62nd Street stands the third home of the:

3. **Knickerbocker Club,** which looks a lot like the big private houses that once characterized the avenue. The Georgian brick Knickerbocker, completed in 1915, was the work of a firm called Delano and Aldrich, a favorite of high society in the early 20th century. It retains a very pedigreed image. Ernest Hemingway, looking for peace and quiet, rented an apartment here in 1959, and stayed for about a year.

The next block up is 63rd Street and just north of it you'll see:

4. **820 Fifth Avenue,** one of the earliest apartment houses built hereabouts and still one of the best. Built in 1916, it houses only one apartment on each floor, with five fireplaces and seven bathrooms in each.

Continue northward on Fifth Avenue to 64th Street. Cross the avenue and walk just inside Central Park for a look at:

5. **The Arsenal,** built in 1848 when this neighborhood was distant and deserted. Now housing zoo administration offices, the structure was once a bunkhouse for Civil War troops. Note the eagle over the door and the pyramids made of cannonballs on the facade. The **Central Park Zoo** is right behind the building.

Head back onto Fifth Avenue. Opposite the park, at the southeast corner of 64th Street, is the former mansion of coal magnate Edward Berwind. If you've seen the mansions in Newport, Rhode Island, you've probably already seen Mr. Berwind's summer house, the Elms. His New York

The Upper East Side

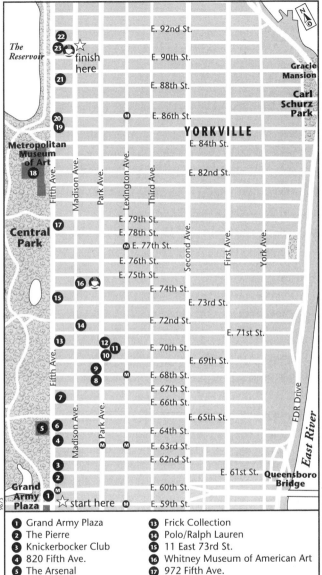

1 Grand Army Plaza	**13** Frick Collection
2 The Pierre	**14** Polo/Ralph Lauren
3 Knickerbocker Club	**15** 11 East 73rd St.
4 820 Fifth Ave.	**16** Whitney Museum of American Art
5 The Arsenal	**17** 972 Fifth Ave.
6 3 East 64th St.	**18** Metropolitan Museum of Art
7 Home of Ulysses S. Grant	**19** Home of Jackie Kennedy Onassis
8 58 East 68th St.	**20** 86th Street
9 680 Park Ave.	**21** Guggenheim Museum
10 Union Club	**22** Cooper-Hewitt National Design Museum
11 East 70th Street	**23** Convent of the Sacred Heart
12 Asia Society	

residence dates from 1896 and has been preserved as cooperative apartments.

Head east on 64th Street toward Madison Avenue. This is a particularly handsome East Side block, lined with architectural extravaganzas. Note in particular:

6. **3 East 64th Street,** an opulent Beaux Arts mansion built in 1903 for the daughter of Mrs. William B. Astor. The house was designed by Warren and Wetmore, the firm responsible for Grand Central Terminal, and it now houses the Consulate General of India. Also worthy of admiration on this block are nos. 11, 16, 19, and 20.

At the corner of Madison Avenue and 64th Street, turn left and proceed two blocks north to 66th Street. Note the rather fantastical apartment house built in 1900 on the northeast corner of 66th and Madison, then turn left (west) off Madison onto 66th Street, heading back toward Fifth Avenue.

Among the many notable houses on this block is the magnificent French Renaissance–style house at 5 East 66th Street, with its heavy wooden doors and its elegant stonework detail. It's now home to the Lotos Club, which is dedicated to literature and the fine arts, but it was built in 1900 as the city residence of William J. Schiefflin.

Next door, at 3 East 66th Street, you'll find the:

7. **Home of President Ulysses S. Grant,** where he lived from 1881 to 1885. Forced to declare bankruptcy after a disastrous presidency that was marred by scandal, the former Civil War hero retired here to spend his last years penning his personal memoirs. Though he was battling cancer, Grant managed to hang on just long enough to complete his autobiography, which won favorable literary reviews and earned his family half a million dollars.

Now double back to Madison Avenue, turn left, and continue north for two more blocks, stopping to browse in any of the boutiques that catch your eye. There's Nicole Miller; Baby Guess for the upscale infant; La Perla for lovely lingerie; Emanuel Ungaro; Godiva, which offers a few café tables for lingering over coffee and a decadent truffle; Monaco for cashmere; and Peter Fox for the priciest boots this side of Dallas. At 68th Street, turn right (east) toward

Park Avenue. One of the best houses on this block is:

8. **58 East 68th Street,** on the southwest corner of the intersection with Park Avenue. The house was originally built in 1919 for Harold J. Pratt, son of Rockefeller partner Charles Pratt. Its construction signaled a major departure for this member of the famously close-knit Pratts. His three brothers all built mansions in Brooklyn opposite their father's. Virtually the entire family summered together in a complex of adjoining estates on Long Island. But 58 East 68th Street is in Manhattan, with no other Pratts in sight.

Walk to the north side of 68th Street to:

9. **680 Park Avenue,** a neo-Federal town house, build in 1909 to 1911 for banker Percy Rivington Pyne and designed by McKim, Mead, and White. Its materials and scale established a character that was followed by the architects of all the subsequent houses on this Park Avenue blockfront. The building was occupied by the Soviet Mission to the United Nations from 1948 to 1963, and Soviet premier Nikita Krushchev waved to curious crowds from its Park Avenue balcony during his famous shoe-banging visit to the U.N.

The Marquesa de Cuevas acquired the property in 1965 and saved it from the wrecker's ball by presenting it to the Americas Society, which still occupies the premises today. The society is the only national not-for-profit institution devoted to educating U.S. citizens about their Western Hemisphere neighbors. Art exhibitions and cultural programs on Latin American and Canadian affairs are open to the public.

Head north on Park Avenue to 69th Street, where, on the northeast corner, is the:

10. **Union Club,** designed in 1932 to house New York's oldest club. On the other side of 69th Street is Hunter College. Continue east toward Lexington Avenue, noting en route 117 East 69th Street, a prototypical not-so-small private East Side house with beautiful stained-glass panels around the door.

When you arrive at Lexington Avenue, turn left and walk one block uptown to 70th Street. Then turn left again and head back toward Park Avenue along:

11. **East 70th Street,** which presents a succession of elegant houses, each more beautiful than the next. Some consider this the finest street in New York; it's certainly near the top of my list. Note in particular no. 125, a post–World War II mansion built for Paul Mellon in a French provincial style.

When you arrive at the Park Avenue end of the block, note the modern building on the northeast corner housing the:

12. **Asia Society,** which offers workshops, lectures, films, and performances on Asian culture. Major art exhibitions, both ancient and contemporary, are held in the galleries; admission is charged.

Now continue across the street and note **720 Park Avenue,** on the northwest corner of the intersection. This is a prime example of the sort of swanky, enormous apartment building that lured former mansion dwellers away from their private houses. The upper floors of buildings like no. 720 often contain apartments with three or four floors and dozens of rooms.

Cross Park Avenue and continue west toward Fifth Avenue. You'll pass a lovely courtyard and pool, surrounded by stately black iron gates, before reaching the entrance to the:

13. **Frick Collection,** housed in the 1914 mansion of steel magnate Henry Clay Frick and very evocative of the Gilded Age. The beautiful classic garden overlooking 70th Street was built in 1977. Inside, the Frick has a notable collection of paintings—Gainsboroughs, Titians, and other treasures acquired by the Fricks over 40 years—as well as many original furnishings. Frick intended that the house, occupying a full blockfront on Fifth Avenue, be converted to a museum after his death.

The Frick Collection is open Tuesday through Saturday from 10am to 6pm, and on Sundays from 1 to 6pm (it's closed on holidays). Admission is charged; no children under 10 are admitted (children from ages 10 to 16 must be accompanied by an adult to enter).

Turn right at the corner of Fifth Avenue, passing a beautiful colonnade on the side of the Frick building. Continue two blocks north, and turn right onto 72nd Street, heading toward Madison Avenue and:

14. **Polo/Ralph Lauren.** This showcase store, housed in a renovated mansion that dates to 1895, looks for all the world like an English country place, complete with working fireplaces, Persian rugs, the antiques, and a grand baronial staircase. The store is closed on Sundays.

Take Madison Avenue up a block to 73rd Street, passing One Night Stand, which rents fabulous designer evening wear for women, and Yumi Katsura, a boutique showcasing exquisite wedding gowns for the well-to-do bride. Detour to your left on 73rd Street (past the adorable La Maison du Chocolat) to see:

15. **11 East 73rd Street,** a particularly sumptuous house built in 1903 by McKim, Mead, and White for Joseph Pulitzer, the Hungarian-born publisher of a once-famous but long-vanished newspaper called the *New York World.* Pulitzer rarely lived in this house because of an extreme sensitivity to sound. At one time, it contained a special soundproofed room (mounted on ball bearings, no less) to prevent vibrations. When he died in 1911, Pulitzer bequeathed $2 million to the Columbia Graduate School of Journalism, whose trustees bestow the Pulitzer Prizes, annual awards for outstanding achievement in journalism, literature, drama, and musical composition.

Retrace your steps back to Madison Avenue and turn left. You're now in the heart of Madison Avenue gallery country—take time to browse in any of the galleries that catch your eye for the remainder of the tour. You may also want to poke your head into Books and Co., a lovely bookstore on the east side of Madison, just north of 74th Street. Just above it stands the Store Next Door (to the Whitney Museum, that is), with a wonderfully whimsical selection of cards, magnets, T-shirts, clocks, calendars, jewelry, and other creative gifts. On the southeast corner of 75th and Madison, you'll see the:

16. **Whitney Museum of American Art,** housed in a modern structure designed in 1966 by Marcel Breuer. The Whitney contains an impressive collection that concentrates on 20th-century American art, with paintings that reflect historical trends from naturalism to pop art and abstract expressionism. Roy Lichtenstein, Georgia O'Keeffe, and

Edward Hopper are just a few of the artists represented here. Museum hours are Wednesdays and Friday through Sunday from 11am to 6pm, and Thursdays from 1 to 8pm. Admission is charged.

Take a Break Inside the Whitney is the perfect place to stop for a bite—**Sarabeth's at the Whitney,** located on the lower level, is much more than your average museum cafeteria. I had a terrific smoked-turkey sandwich with Vermont cheddar cheese; you might be tempted by the grilled vegetable sandwich on focaccia with shiitake mushrooms and eggplant. Sarabeth's is also known for its scrumptious desserts (like the crème brûlée or the chocolate mousse cake with Saboyan) and for its extensive brunch choices (such as pumpkin waffles or granola with fruit, honey, and yogurt).

Though it's housed in the museum, you don't have to pay admission charges to reach the café. You will, however, get a chance to admire one of Alexander Calder's most famous and most disarming works—*Calder's Wonderful Circus,* with performers and animals shaped from wire and scraps of cloth.

Leave the museum and continue uptown on Madison Avenue. At 76th Street, you'll pass one of New York's grand old hotels, **the Carlyle,** which has counted two presidents among its famous guests—Harry Truman and John F. Kennedy. On the left side of Madison, you might like to explore Tenzing & Pema, with a great selection of toys and games, from dog puppets to magnetic 3-D globe puzzles. The west side of Madison Avenue from 76th to 77th Streets is lined with a procession of intriguing contemporary galleries: David Findlay, The Pace Collection, and the Weintraub Gallery. Above 77th Street, you'll see fabulously ornate cakes in the window of Sant Ambroeus, an authentic Italian bakery, a good place for a gelato break.

Turn left when you reach 79th Street and return to Fifth Avenue. There's an impressive row of buildings here—everything from French château–style structures to neo-Georgian town houses. When you reach the corner of Fifth Avenue, turn left for a look at:

17. **972 Fifth Avenue,** which lies between 78th and 79th Streets. It is now the French Embassy's Cultural Services Office, but it was built in 1906 as a wedding present for Payne Whitney by his doting (and childless) rich uncle, Oliver Payne, a Civil War officer and one of the benefactors who helped to found Cornell's Medical College. This McKim, Mead, and White opus cost $1 million and was the talk of the town in its day.

Next door, on the corner of 78th Street, is the classic French-style mansion of tobacco millionaire James B. Duke (as in Duke University). His daughter Doris occupied the house intermittently until 1957, when she donated it to New York University. NYU now operates it as a fine arts institute.

Now turn around and walk north on Fifth Avenue (pausing to note the wonderful stone owl perched above the door of 973 Fifth Avenue). On your left at 82nd Street is the grand entrance to the:

18. **Metropolitan Museum of Art,** one of the world's greatest cultural institutions. The block of 82nd Street that faces the museum's mammoth staircase almost acts as a sort of formal court.

The Met's collection is the largest in the Western Hemisphere, including an Egytian wing that boasts tens of thousands of objects. Its Temple of Dendur, circa 15 B.C. from Lower Nubia, was shipped piece by piece to the Met and painstakingly reconstructed.

Museum hours are Sundays and Tuesday through Thursday from 9:30am to 5:15pm, Fridays and Saturdays from 9:30am to 8:45pm. There's a suggested contribution if you enter and decide to browse for a while; however, it would take a lifetime to see all of the Met's treasures, so it might be best to save it for another day and merely admire the exterior for now.

Continue uptown to 85th Street. No. 1040 Fifth Avenue was for many years the:

19. **Home of Jacqueline Kennedy Onassis.** After her husband's assassination, she moved here so that Caroline could attend school at nearby Sacred Heart. The former

first lady adored New York, and was often spotted strolling nearby in her beloved Central Park. After her death from cancer in 1994, hundreds of mourners gathered outside this building, many leaving flowers on the sidewalk in her memory.

Continue uptown to:

20. **86th Street.** The big brick-and-limestone mansion on the southeast corner of Fifth Avenue and 86th Street was built in 1914 for William Star Miller. It was to this house that Mrs. Cornelius Vanderbilt retreated in 1944 when her famous 640 Fifth Avenue house was sold. No. 640 Fifth Avenue was located down on 51st Street and was the first of a concentration of family houses that at one time caused Fifth Avenue in the 1950s to be called "Vanderbilt Alley." By 1944, Mrs. V. was pretty much alone down there, surrounded by ghosts of the Vanderbilt past and lots of noisy traffic and new office buildings. The exile to 86th Street appears, at least from the look of this house, to have been comfortable, anyway.

Two blocks further up Fifth Avenue is the:

21. **Guggenheim Museum,** between 88th and 89th Streets, whose building piques just as much interest as the collection of modern masterpieces it houses. Designed by Frank Lloyd Wright in 1959, it set off a storm of architectural controversy when it was built. Nowadays, New Yorkers have grown to think of the building as a treasured landmark—so much so that the addition of new exhibition space sparked an outcry among those who felt that the city's only building designed by Wright should never be altered. The structure has a unique spiral shape; visitors generally take an elevator to the top floor, then walk down the ramp, viewing the works of art hung along the curved walls.

The Guggenheim's hours are Sunday through Wednesday from 10am to 6pm, Friday and Saturday from 10am to 8pm. Admission is charged. Check out the museum store's T-shirts, gifts, prints, and books.

Uptown from the Guggenheim, between 90th and 91st Streets, is another major sight, the:

22. **Cooper-Hewitt National Design Museum.** Under the auspices of the Smithsonian Institution, it is housed in the former Andrew Carnegie mansion. Built in 1901, this Georgianesque palace originally shared the neighborhood with squatters' shanties and roaming pigs. By the time the squatters were gone and the streets were built up with fine houses, Carnegie was dead. His widow lived in the house until 1949.

Across 91st Street from the main entrance to the Cooper-Hewitt is the:

23. **Convent of the Sacred Heart,** occupying what was once the largest private house ever built in Manhattan. Financier Otto Kahn bought the property from Andrew Carnegie in 1913, and construction of his mansion was completed in 1918. Closely resembling its model, the papal chancellery in Rome, the house is currently undergoing a major restoration. Other houses on this 91st Street block, notably nos. 7 and 9, are almost as grand.

Take 91st Street east to Madison Avenue and turn right (downtown) if you'd like to end the tour with a pick-me-up.

Winding Down   At the southwest corner of Madison Avenue and 91st Street is **Jackson Hole.** Many New Yorkers argue that Jackson Hole flips the best burgers in the city—and there's no denying that you get a lot for your money. In addition to huge, juicy burgers, Jackson Hole offers omelets, honey-dipped fried chicken, sandwiches, salads, and great desserts. Forget about your cholesterol count and enjoy. Open daily.

BROOKLYN HEIGHTS

Start: Borough Hall.
Subway: Take the N, R, 2, or 3 to Borough Hall.
Finish: Montague Terrace.
Time: Approximately 3 hours.
Best Time: Weekends.

Brooklyn Heights, with its gracious brownstones and serene, tree-lined streets, is all too often overlooked by tourists. Some misguided souls might even think that the only thing to see out here is the view of the Manhattan skyline across the river. They're in for a pleasant surprise, for they'll discover historic sites, such as the spot where George Washington met with his war council as he battled the British; literary haunts, such as the homes of Norman Mailer and Arthur Miller; ethnic restaurants; 19th-century churches; and hundreds of homes that predate the Civil War, many with backyard gardens in bloom.

Once a rural farming village populated by Dutch settlers, Brooklyn Heights came into its own when Robert Fulton's ferry began making the run to and from lower Manhattan in the early 1800s. The ferry brought with it a wave of prosperous city dwellers eager to buy suburban homes, many of them wealthy

Protestant bankers and shipping magnates who worked in Manhattan's financial district or at the seaport.

In the years leading up to the Civil War, Brooklyn Heights became a leading center for the abolitionist movement, and its most prominent church, the Plymouth Church of the Pilgrims, was a major stop on the Underground Railroad. From this pulpit, Henry Ward Beecher became the most acclaimed preacher of his day; Abraham Lincoln once referred to him as "the greatest orator since St. Paul." Another neighborhood resident who profoundly affected American thought in the 1800s was Walt Whitman, once the editor of the *Brooklyn Eagle.* He had the type set for his groundbreaking volume of poetry, *Leaves of Grass,* in a neighborhood print shop that was long ago demolished. (Whitman, also an ardent abolitionist, worked tending the wounded during the Civil War, and his poem *O Captain, My Captain* was written as a tribute to Lincoln.)

As you stroll along the route laid out below, you'll see that Brooklyn Heights has never ceased to attract writers and intellectuals.

● ● ● ● ● ● ● ● ● ● ● ● ● ● ● ● ● ●

Start at Court and Remsen Streets, where:

1. **Borough Hall** sits crowned with an impressive cupola. This imposing structure was completed in 1849, just as New York City's shipping industry began to boom with the opening of the Erie Canal, and Brooklyn was transformed from a farming village into a major center for commerce. Borough Hall was a tremendous source of pride for the neighborhood, and it served as Brooklyn's City Hall until 1898, when Brooklyn was incorporated into the City of New York.

   If you're taking the tour on a Tuesday or a Saturday, you'll run across the **Greenmarket Farmer's Market,** which is held year-round. I last came by on a Saturday in autumn and sampled some hot mulled cider while checking out the vendors' offerings: spices, plants, fresh fish, baked goods, and farm-fresh apples, pumpkins, and other produce.

   Now backtrack west to Clinton Street and turn left; stroll south on Clinton for several blocks. On the right side of the street, just before you reach Atlantic Avenue, is a charming store called **Two for the Pot,** at 200 Clinton Street. Its shelves are full of glass cannisters containing teas and spices; you can search here for a coffeemaker or the perfect barbecue sauce.

Straight ahead of you lies:

2. **Atlantic Avenue,** the center of New York's Arab community. In the 1940s, construction on the new Brooklyn Battery Tunnel demolished much of Manhattan's Arab neighborhood, and many of its residents resettled along this avenue. Today, this area is home to Syrians, Lebanese, Palestinians, and Yemenis, and the avenue is lined with Arab coffeehouses, bakeries, and emporiums.

Turn left and wander for a block or two before doubling back to continue the rest of the tour, which leads off to your right. The **Damascus Bakery,** at 195 Atlantic Avenue, has been around since 1933 and is the place to buy freshly baked Syrian flatbreads in plain, garlic, onion, whole wheat, and other varieties. Take a peek inside the **Sahadi Importing Company,** at no. 187, for an exotic selection of dried fruits, freshly prepared take-home foods, olives, feta cheese, and more. At no. 170 is the **Oriental Pastry and Grocery,** where you can purchase desserts such as Turkish delight or all the ingredients to whip up your own sugary concoctions.

Take a Break   No trip to Atlantic Avenue would be complete without lunch at **Tripoli,** at no. 156 (tel. 718/596-5800), an authentic Lebanese restaurant where you can sample some terrific, moderately priced Middle Eastern fare. Slide into one of the ornately carved wooden chairs and take your pick from the menu, which includes the Tripoli Maza, a sampler platter of hummus, baba ghanoush, falafel, and salad. In addition to standbys such as shish kebab and couscous, there are more creative entrées, such as *abanegh,* sautéed spinach, lamb, and pine nuts, served with rice and yogurt. Vegetarians will find no fewer than 10 entrée choices on the menu. You can have a satisfying meal here for less than $10. Tripoli is open daily from 11am to 11pm, with live music on weekend nights. A highly recommended spot.

From Atlantic Avenue, turn right onto Henry Street, then left onto State Street. The very next right turn will bring you to:

Brooklyn Heights

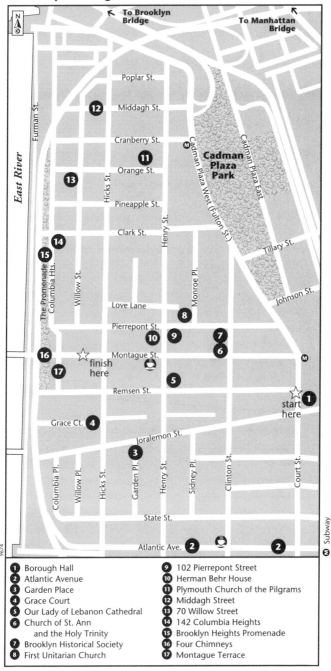

To Brooklyn Bridge

To Manhattan Bridge

East River

Furman St.

Poplar St.
Middagh St.
Cranberry St.
Orange St.
Pineapple St.
Clark St.

Hicks St.

Henry St.

Cadman Plaza West (Fulton St.)

Cadman Plaza East

Cadman Plaza Park

Tillary St.

Johnson St.

The Promenade

Columbia Hts.

Willow St.

Monroe Pl.

Love Lane
Pierrepont St.
Montague St.
Remsen St.

finish here

start here

Grace Ct.

Joralemon St.

Columbia Pl.

Willow Pl.

Hicks St.

Garden Pl.

Henry St.

Sidney Pl.

Clinton St.

Court St.

State St.

Atlantic Ave.

Subway

9674

1 Borough Hall
2 Atlantic Avenue
3 Garden Place
4 Grace Court
5 Our Lady of Lebanon Cathedral
6 Church of St. Ann
  and the Holy Trinity
7 Brooklyn Historical Society
8 First Unitarian Church

9 102 Pierrepont Street
10 Herman Behr House
11 Plymouth Church of the Pilgrams
12 Middagh Street
13 70 Willow Street
14 142 Columbia Heights
15 Brooklyn Heights Promenade
16 Four Chimneys
17 Montague Terrace

3. **Garden Place,** a lovely block lined with carriage houses and charming residences. Garden Place ends at Joralemon Street, where you'll turn left before making a right onto Hicks Street. (Hicks Street, by the way, was named after a prominent local farming family—from whose name snobbish city dwellers coined the term "hick" to refer to country and farm folk.) Take the first street branching off to your left, a tranquil little cul-de-sac called:

4. **Grace Court.** At the corner stands Grace Episcopal Church, a Gothic Revival sandstone structure designed in 1847 by Richard Upjohn; it boasts three stained-glass windows by Louis Comfort Tiffany. Arthur Miller owned no. 31 from 1947 to 1951, and it was here that he penned his most famous work, *Death of a Salesman.* If you walk to the end of Grace Court, you'll get a glimpse of the East River and the Manhattan skyline.

Retrace your steps back to Hicks Street and continue north for another block. Now make a right onto Remsen Street. On the right side of the street, take a moment to admire the architectural details on the building at no. 70—low marble columns, stone arches, and, best of all, a delightful row of gargoyles (see if you can spot the bat, the ram, the pig-man, and the lion).

Further along Remsen, at the corner of Henry Street, stands:

5. **Our Lady of Lebanon Cathedral,** also designed by Richard Upjohn. This church, however, was acquired by the Maronite Christians of the Lebanese community in 1944, who incorporated Middle Eastern design touches into the structure. These include a Mediterranean-themed mural over the altar, Arabic-style calligraphic designs bordering the walls and ceiling, and stained-glass windows reminiscent of mosaic patterns. Take a minute to admire the intricate panels at the southern and western portals; they were rescued from the *Normandie,* an ocean liner that burned in 1942. If the church is closed and you're unable to enter, at least you can take a look at the bronze doors on the Henry Street side of the building.

Continue along Remsen to Clinton Street and make a left. One block up, across Montague Street on your left, is the Episcopal:

6. **Church of St. Ann and the Holy Trinity,** built from 1843 to 1847. Its stained-glass windows, created by William Bolton, were among the first made in the United States. St. Ann's has long been one of the most prestigious congregations among the upper middle class of Brooklyn Heights.

Across Clinton Street is a magnificent Italian palazzo-style bank building. It's a branch of Chemical Bank, designed by York & Sawyer, the same architects responsible for the Federal Reserve Bank and the Apple Bank for Savings in Manhattan. Across the street from St. Ann's, notice the wonderful lampposts at the south side of the bank. Above a fierce-looking griffin, turtles poke their heads out on each corner of the bases.

Continue north on Clinton to Pierrepont Street, where you'll make a left. Facing Pierrepont is the:

7. **Brooklyn Historical Society.** The prints and artifacts in the gallery celebrate Brooklyn's history and heritage, from Coney Island to the still-beloved Brooklyn Dodgers (who got their name from the fans' skill at dodging the trolley cars near Ebbets Field). Frequent lectures and special exhibitions explore topics such as Brooklyn firefighters, the immigrant experience, and the Revolutionary War battle fought in Brooklyn. Upstairs is a reading room crammed with a vast collection of maps, photographs, newspapers, and manuscripts. The gallery is open Tuesday through Saturday from noon to 5pm; the library's hours are Tuesday through Saturday from 10am to 4:45pm. Admission is charged; there's a research fee for use of the library that includes entry to the museum.

Continue west along Pierrepont Street. On your right, just past Monroe Place, is the:

8. **First Unitarian Church,** the oldest church building in Brooklyn Heights, consecrated in 1844. It was commissioned by a group of Unitarian merchants who were ostracized by their more conservative Protestant counterparts in New England and came to settle in New York. The church is graced with a series of windows designed by Louis Comfort Tiffany.

Across the street is:

9. **102 Pierrepont Street,** a brownstone where Arthur Miller lived from 1944 to 1947 and where he wrote *All My Sons.* Norman Mailer lived upstairs with his parents; it was here that he produced *The Naked and the Dead.*

    A little further along Pierrepont, just past Henry Street, is the:

10. **Herman Behr House,** a stately residential building designed by Frank Freeman in the Romanesque Revival style. The original structure was enlarged to become the Hotel Palm, before it was reincarnated as a brothel (the roster of tenants underwent a dramatic change when the building was later acquired by the Catholic church). It was eventually sold for conversion to co-op apartments in 1976.

    Now turn right and head north on Henry Street for several blocks. Just past Love Lane stands a tiny **D'Agostino**— it may or may not be the smallest branch of this grocery store chain in New York, but it's certainly the most charming, housed in a town house that's no wider than the average residence. Continue along Henry Street past Clark and Pineapple Streets, before turning left onto Orange Street. On your right stands the:

11. **Plymouth Church of the Pilgrims,** whose exterior appearance is reminiscent of a New England meeting house. The statue in the courtyard beside the church is of Henry Ward Beecher, pastor of the church for more than 40 years in the mid-19th century. One of the most influential figures in the history of Brooklyn Heights, Beecher was a leading abolitionist, as was his sister, Harriet Beecher Stowe, who authored *Uncle Tom's Cabin.* Beecher once brought a slave girl named Pinky before his congregation and auctioned her off to demonstrate the horrors of slavery (the parishioners got the point—they bought her freedom). Plymouth Church was a major stopping point on the Underground Railroad, a network of abolitionists who aided and housed slaves escaping to the North.

    Inside the church before you, Beecher delivered fiery sermons eloquently denouncing slavery. He traveled to England on a speaking tour that was so successful he was credited with turning British public opinion against the

The Hottest Scandal of the 19th Century

Henry Ward Beecher, the world-renowned preacher who served as pastor of Brooklyn's Plymouth Church of the Pilgrims, met his match when he tangled with Victoria Woodhull, and one of the juiciest scandals of the late 19th century ensued. Woodhull and her sister, Tennessee Claflin, both spiritualists, were set up in a brokerage business in 1870 by none other than Commodore Vanderbilt himself. A few months later, the sisters launched publication of *Woodhull and Claflin's Weekly,* a magazine that advocated abortion rights, giving women the vote, and free love; it also ran the first translation of Marx's *Communist Manifesto* to appear in America. After a memorable address to the House Judiciary Committee, Woodhull skyrocketed to prominence in the suffrage movement. Beecher and his sisters, all deeply opposed to women's rights, began to attack Woodhull publicly, denouncing her rather unconventional domestic arrangements.

Woodhull, infuriated, countered with an article in the November 1872 issue of the *Weekly.* "I intend that this article shall burst like a bombshell into the ranks of the moralistic social camp," she wrote—and a bombshell it was. Beecher, at the peak of his influence after the war and the highest-paid preacher in the nation, regularly condemned free love in public—while in private he was carrying on an affair with one of his parishioners, a married woman named Elizabeth Tilton. The issue that exposed him was selling on the streets of New York for $40 a copy within hours.

The scandal did not ruin Beecher, however. In 1875 Tilton's husband sued Beecher for alienation of his wife's affections, and though the trial dragged on for six months, loaded with sensational testimony and followed by every newspaper in the country, the proceedings ended in a hung jury. The crowds flocking to hear the famous preacher only increased, with thousands arriving in Brooklyn in "Beecher boats" every Sunday.

South. When the Civil War ended, Abraham Lincoln asked Beecher to deliver the invocation at the flag-raising ceremony at Fort Sumter.

Though the church will be forever associated with Beecher, other notables who spoke here include Clara Barton, John Greenleaf Whittier, Ralph Waldo Emerson, Booker T. Washington, Charles Dickens, and Mark Twain. Abraham Lincoln once worshiped here as well, and the church also holds a fragment of Plymouth Rock.

Now turn right onto Hicks Street and head north, past Cranberry Street, admiring the handsome brownstones as you pass. Turn left onto:

12. **Middagh Street.** The house that once stood at no. 7 was demolished to accommodate expressway traffic—a tragedy for literary enthusiasts. Carson McCullers, W. H. Auden, and George Davis, the literary editor of *Harper's Bazaar,* set up housekeeping at this address in the early 1940s. (The house's cook was referred to the trio by famed stripper Gypsy Rose Lee.) Jane and Paul Bowles, the latter the author of *The Sheltering Sky,* rented a floor here, and Anaïs Nin, Salvador Dalí, and Aaron Copeland all stopped in at one time or another. Richard Wright took the basement apartment with his family, but only briefly; he found the atmosphere "not a proper environment in which to raise a child."

Take Middagh Street to Willow Street and turn left. Between Pineapple and Orange Streets, you'll come to a magnificent house at:

13. **70 Willow Street.** Truman Capote wrote *In Cold Blood* and *Breakfast at Tiffany's* while he was a tenant in the basement apartment.

Retrace your steps back to Orange Street; take Orange one block west and turn left onto Columbia Heights. The building that once stood at no. 110, now long gone, was the home of Washington Roebling, who changed the face of Brooklyn forever by overseeing construction of the Brooklyn Bridge.

His father, John, designed the bridge and began the project, but his foot was crushed while he was surveying the site; the elder Roebling contracted tetanus and died. Washington vowed to fulfill his father's dream and began to drive himself at a furious pace.

Washington Roebling insisted on diving into the East River with the workmen as the pilings were put in place, and he, like many of the construction workers, fell victim to the bends. Even after his health was ruined, he continued to direct the project from his sickbed, using binoculars or a telescope to keep an eye on its progress. The world's longest suspension bridge when it was completed in 1883, it was the first link over the East River between Manhattan and Brooklyn. It is a marvel of engineering, with magnificent stone archways and heavy steel cables that appear as delicate as cobwebs. British art historian Kenneth Clark once commented that "all modern New York, heroic New York, started with the Brooklyn Bridge."

Later, in the 1920s, poet Hart Crane lived in no. 110. He was moved by Roebling's efforts, and so inspired by the view that he produced an epic poem entitled *The Bridge.* Crane once commented that it was "the most superb piece of construction in the modern world, I'm sure, with strings of light crossing it like glowing worms as the Ls and surface cars pass each other going and coming." Crane often stumbled home drunk across the bridge after attending parties in the Village; he was often met by John Dos Passos, who also lived in no. 110, and who usually implored him to go home and sleep it off.

Head south and look for:

14. **142 Columbia Heights,** where author Norman Mailer has lived for many years.

Now, near Clark Street, take the path on your right that leads to the:

15. **Brooklyn Heights Promenade** (also referred to as the Esplanade). As you stroll south through the promenade, a breathtaking view of the Manhattan skyline will stretch before you, dominated by the twin towers of the World Trade Center. You'll see the Woolworth Building, the Brooklyn Bridge, and the tall ships moored near Pier 17 of South Street Seaport. To the left of Manhattan, you'll see the Statue of Liberty holding her torch over New York Harbor. Nearby lies Ellis Island; 12 million people from every corner of the world passed through the immigration facility here, hoping to begin a better life in America.

Wander south and take in the view at your leisure; if you're here on a pleasant summer afternoon, the promenade will be lined with artists and vendors, making for a wonderful stroll.

Leave the promenade near the south end at Montague Street. As you do so, you'll pass a plaque where the:

16. **Four Chimneys** once stood. You may not have known it, but Brooklyn was the site of one of the first battles of the Revolutionary War, in which British forces unleashed a surprise attack on American forts in August 1776. This plaque marks the site of the house in which George Washington stayed during the battle and in which a Council of War was held. Washington almost lost the entire Continental Army in Brooklyn by neglecting to block off a small road near Flatbush. The British surrounded the rebellious colonists, and only a blanket of fog allowed Washington and his troops to escape to Manhattan.

To your right as you leave the promenade is:

17. **Montague Terrace,** boasting a row of town houses built in the 1880s. W. H. Auden occupied no. 1, and in the early 1930s, Thomas Wolfe completed work on *Of Time and the River* while living at no. 5. In 1934, an article appeared that mentioned no. 5 as Wolfe's address; he was so besieged by fans that he was forced to leave Brooklyn and move into a hotel.

Wind up your tour by wandering east along Montague Street. Browse in the shops or stop in one of the many cafés and eateries you'll pass on your way back to the subway at Borough Hall.

Winding Down Montague Street is the heart of Brooklyn Heights, and it offers numerous places to stop for a bite, whether you're craving sushi, enchiladas, or sweet-and-sour shrimp. A longtime favorite in the neighborhood is the **Montague Street Saloon,** at no. 122 (tel. 718/522-6770), an informal pub serving inexpensive burgers, salads, omelets, and sandwiches. Try the blackened catfish, the veggie stir-fry, or Lisa's chicken sandwich, topped with melted mozzarella. All go well with a bottle of Brooklyn lager, one of the many varieties of beer available here.

ESSENTIALS &
RECOMMENDED READING

To the first-time visitor, New York can be overwhelming. But there is, believe it or not, a method to the madness. The city's layout is sensible and easy to grasp. If you take just a few minutes to figure out the lay of the land, you'll soon be able to negotiate your way around like a native.

ORIENTATION

Main Arteries & Streets Laid out on a grid system, Manhattan is the easiest of the boroughs to negotiate. Avenues run north (uptown) and south (downtown), while the streets run east to west (crosstown) with Fifth Avenue as the East Side/West Side demarcation. Broadway runs north to south diagonally across the grid.

Both avenues and streets are numbered consecutively, streets from south to north (1st Street is downtown just above Houston Street), and avenues from east to west, from First Avenue near the East River to Twelfth Avenue near the Hudson River. The only exceptions are the three named avenues on the East

Side: Madison (next to Fifth Avenue), Park, and Lexington. Sixth Avenue is also called the Avenue of the Americas.

A few West Side avenues acquire new names as they move uptown: Eighth Avenue becomes Central Park West above 59th Street, Ninth Avenue becomes Columbus Avenue above 69th Street, and Tenth Avenue becomes Amsterdam above 72nd Street.

This pattern changes in the older downtown sections below 14th Street on the West Side, and below Houston Street on the East Side. Downtown streets have names rather than numbers, and in the oldest sections, streets follow the outlines of original cowpaths and old village streets. They twist and turn in no defined fashion and give such neighborhoods as Greenwich Village, Chinatown, and the Wall Street area their particular charm, but they are not as easy to negotiate.

Finding An Address   To find the nearest cross street on an avenue address, drop the last digit of the number of the address and divide the remaining number by two. Then add or subtract the appropriate number from the list below.

For example, if you were trying to locate 645 Fifth Avenue, you would drop the 5, leaving 64. Then you would divide 64 by 2, leaving 32. According to the list below, you would then add 20. Thus 645 Fifth Avenue is at about 52nd Street.

Avenue A, B, C, or D	add 3
First Avenue	add 3
Second Avenue	add 3
Third Avenue	add 10
Fourth Avenue (Park Avenue South)	add 8
Fifth Avenue	
1 to 200	add 13
201 to 400	add 16
401 to 600	add 18
601 to 775	add 20
776 to 1286	cancel last figure and subtract 18
Sixth Avenue	subtract 12
Seventh Avenue below Central Park	add 12
Eighth Avenue below Central Park	add 10

Ninth Avenue	add 13
Tenth Avenue	add 14
Eleventh Avenue	add 15
Amsterdam Avenue	add 60
(Tenth Avenue above 72nd Street)	
Broadway	
1 to 754	below 8th Street
754 to 858	subtract 29
858 to 958	subtract 25
Above 1000	subtract 31
Central Park West	divide number
(Eighth Avenue above 59th Street)	by 10 and add 60
Columbus Avenue	add 60
(Ninth Avenue above 69th Street)	
Lexington Avenue	add 22
Madison Avenue	add 26
Park Avenue	add 35
Riverside Drive	divide number by 10 and add 72
West End Avenue	add 60
(Eleventh Avenue above 57th Street)	

All east-west street addresses in New York are counted from Fifth Avenue and increase in number as they move away from Fifth Avenue. Thus the address 2 West 44th Street would denote a building on 44th Street just a few steps to the west of Fifth Avenue; 56 West 44th Street would indicate a building that is even farther west, and so on. The address 12 East 45th Street would denote a building just a little to the east of Fifth Avenue, while 324 East 45th Street would indicate a building on 45th Street that is much farther east of Fifth Avenue.

GETTING AROUND

By Subway   Despite the noise and occasional discomfort, especially during the hottest days of summer, the subway is the quickest, cheapest, and most efficient way to move around the city. I recommend that every visitor ride the subway at least once: If you haven't ridden the subway, you haven't seen New York.

Tokens allow you to ride anywhere on the extensive system, and are obtained at token booths inside the stations. Purchase tokens with small bills; anything larger than a $20 bill will not be accepted.

To the stranger, the system might appear extremely complex and mysterious, so the first thing to do is to obtain a good map, available free at most token booths.

A number of subway lines run through Manhattan. Once the subway was separated into several systems, but today there is only one metropolitan system. The lines are the Seventh Avenue/Broadway line (1, 2, 3, and 9 trains), the Eighth Avenue line (A, C, and E trains), the Sixth Avenue line (B, D, F, and Q trains), the BMT (formerly Brooklyn-Manhattan Transit, still known by its acronym; N, R, J, M, and Z trains), and the Lexington Avenue line (4, 5, and 6 trains). Three subway lines run crosstown: the Grand Central–Times Square shuttle, the Flushing line (7 train), and the Carnarsie–14th Street line (L train). Each train is clearly numbered or lettered, indicating its specific route.

There are many crossover points from line to line; these will be indicated on your subway map. Most lines, as they pass through Midtown, stop at roughly similar cross streets: for example, all lines stop at 59th, 42nd, 33rd/34th, 23rd, and 14th Streets on their respective avenues and routes.

The subway is not difficult to negotiate and is a great time saver. Try not to ride during rush hours—8 to 9:30am and 4:30 to 6pm. Pushing and shoving is the rule then—as at most other times—but at rush hour there are at least a hundred people per car pushing and shoving (feels more like a thousand).

To avoid waiting in line to buy tokens, purchase a 10-pack. Tokens can also be used on the bus.

It is not a particularly good idea to ride very late at night. If you do, avoid empty cars and stand in the clearly designated waiting area of the station. Transit police officers patrol the trains at all times, and the conductor rides in either one of the center cars in a tiny compartment. Some station entrances are closed, and these are marked with a red light; open entrances are marked with a green light.

Do not hesitate to ask questions. Subway personnel (token sellers, conductors, transit police officers) are the best sources of information on exactly which train goes where—and how to negotiate the maze of underground passageways to find the train you're looking for, or to the exit to the street.

By Bus   The bus is the most interesting way to travel and routes are not hard to understand. Buses require exact change in coins; the driver does not make change or take bills. Subway tokens may also be used. Transfers are free.

Virtually every avenue in Manhattan has buses that go either up or down the entire length of that avenue, in one direction since most of the avenues have one-way traffic restrictions. Buses go north (uptown) only on First Avenue, Third Avenue, Park Avenue (to 40th Street only), Madison Avenue, Sixth Avenue (Avenue of the Americas), Eighth Avenue, and Tenth Avenue.

Buses go south (downtown) only on Second Avenue, Lexington Avenue, Fifth Avenue, Broadway (below 59th Street), Seventh Avenue (below 59th Street), and Ninth Avenue.

Along York Avenue, Riverside Drive, and Broadway and Central Park West above 59th Street, buses go in both directions (uptown and downtown).

There are also a number of crosstown buses that go east or west across the entire island. Buses go east on 8th Street, 50th Street, and 65th Street. (*Important note:* This last bus travels along 65th Street on the West Side of Manhattan; after it crosses Central Park to the East Side, it continues along 65th Street to Madison Avenue, turns north for three blocks and continues east.) Buses go west only on 9th Street, 49th Street, and 67th Street. (*Another important note:* This last bus travels along 67th Street on the East Side of Manhattan only; after it crosses Central Park to the West Side, it continues its westbound route on 66th Street.)

Buses go in both directions (east and west) on 14th Street, 23rd Street, 34th Street, 42nd Street, 57th Street, 59th Street, 79th Street, 86th Street, 96th Street, 116th Street, 125th Street, 145th Street, and 155th Street.

Free transfers can only be used where routes intersect (ask for your transfer when you pay your fare as bus drivers often get cranky if asked later).

By Taxi   Obviously the most convenient way to travel around town is by cab, but it's not cheap. As of this writing, there is a

50¢ surcharge tacked on each fare from 8pm to 6am. Of course you are also expected to tip, but don't let any driver intimidate you—give around 15% on all fares.

On short rides, if a group of people hop a cab together it can often cost less than taking a subway.

Although it's usually easy enough to walk out and hail a passing cab, there may be occasions when you'd prefer door-to-door service. Check the *Yellow Pages* under the heading "Taxicab Service" for radio-dispatched cabs, which operate on regular meter rates, though sometimes there's an extra charge if you reserve in advance.

Cabs are hard to come by during morning and evening rush hours, and furthermore any trip at these times will cost you a fortune in waiting time. It's also hard to find a cab in inclement weather.

Avoid gypsy cabs. These cabs do not have a medallion on top, many have a battered appearance, and they offer somewhat questionable service. There are, however, some fine private-car services with radio-dispatched late-model sedans. If you find yourself in an area not serviced by regular yellow cabs, ask a local person for a recommendation or check the *Yellow Pages* under "Car Service" or "Taxis." Ask for the rate when booking service.

By Car Try to avoid driving in Manhattan. Drivers are aggressive, street parking is close to impossible, and garage parking is expensive. Illegally parked cars are towed, and you will have to pay a stiff fine to recover your vehicle. People in New York have been known to have fistfights over street-side parking places. If you're very lucky, you may catch someone leaving a spot; otherwise, you'll need to keep circling. Don't wait to see a car pulling out. Watch for telltale signs—a person reaching into a pocket for keys, opening a car door, or walking purposefully toward a vehicle.

The main office of the **American Automobile Association (AAA)** in Manhattan is at Broadway and 62nd Street (tel. 757-2000).

The major **national car rental** companies, such as Avis, Budget, National, and Hertz, all have branches in Manhattan, but be prepared for sky-high rates.

FAST FACTS **New York**

American Express American Express Travel Services has several offices around Manhattan, including the following: 150 East 42nd Street (tel. 687-3700); in Bloomingdales, at Lexington Avenue and 59th Street (tel. 705-3171); in Macy's, at Herald Square (tel. 695-8075); and in the World Financial Center (tel. 640-5130).

Area Code The area code for Manhattan and the Bronx is 212; for Queens, Staten Island, and Brooklyn it's 718; for Long Island it's 516; for Westchester and Rockland counties it's 914; for suburban Connecticut it's 203; and for New Jersey it's 201, 908, or 609.

Bookstores It would be impossible to list all of New York's bookstores here, so what follows is only a very abbreviated list of some of the more interesting offerings: Applause Theatre & Cinema Books, 211 West 71st Street, between Broadway and West End Avenue (tel. 496-7511); Gotham Bookmart, 41 West 47th Street, between Fifth and Sixth Avenues (tel. 719-4448); Murder, Inc., 2486 Broadway, between 92nd and 93rd Streets (tel. 362-8905); the Strand, 828 Broadway, at 12th Street (tel. 473-1452); and A Different Light, 151 West 19th Street, between Sixth and Seventh Avenues (tel. 989-4850).

Business Hours Standard office hours are 9am to 5pm. Banks in Manhattan keep relatively short hours, closing on most weekdays at 3 or 3:30pm. Department stores are usually open until 6pm, with late closings (usually around 8:30pm on Mondays and Thursdays). Bars and restaurants keep late hours, with a good number of eateries open around the clock.

Climate New York's weather is nothing if not fickle. In winter the wind can be bitterly cold or you could be in for mild sunny skies. (Summers tend to be universally humid and muggy.) Your best bet is to dress in layers and to keep an eye on each day's weather forecast.

Newspapers/Magazines New York has four major daily newspapers, the *New York Times,* the *Daily News,* the *New York Post,* and *New York Newsday.* The Friday "Weekend" and the Sunday "Arts and Leisure" sections of the *Times* are especially good resources. Weekly publications with good entertainment and cultural listings include the *New Yorker, New York* magazine, and the *Village Voice* (which is particularly strong for music, cheap events, freebies, and off- and off-off-Broadway performances).

Restrooms   Many restaurants reserve their restrooms for customers' use only; you can generally just buy a soda or a cup of coffee to get around this restriction. All the major department stores are good bets, and you can also use the facilities in the lobbies of most of the better hotels.

Safety   New York's reputation as a dangerous city is not entirely undeserved, but by using common sense you can minimize your chances of becoming a crime victim. Some areas should be avoided entirely at night, including Harlem, the section of the East Village known as "Alphabet City," and the Lower East Side. The subways aren't recommended for late-night travel.

Taxes   New York sales tax is $8^1/_4\%$.

Tourist Information   Stop by the New York Convention and Visitors Bureau at 2 Columbus Circle (West 59th Street and Broadway; tel. 397-8222), open from 9am to 6pm Monday through Friday, 10am to 3pm weekends and holidays. The staff is knowledgeable and the bureau offers a wealth of brochures and information on attractions, dining, accommodations, transportation, services, shopping, and special events.

Transit Information   For bus or subway information and routes, call 718/330-1234, a 24-hour number.

RECOMMENDED READING

Note: In addition to the below-listed, you'll find a number of interesting books mentioned in the Greenwich Village Literary Tours (nos. 5 and 6).

General

Alleman, Richard, *The Movie Lover's Guide to New York* (Harper & Row, 1988).

Bayles, W. H., *Old Taverns of New York* (Gordon Press, 1977).

Beard, Rick, and Berlowitz, Leslie C., *Greenwich Village: Culture and Counterculture* (Rutgers University Press, 1993).

Black, Mary, *Old New York in Early Photographs: Eighteen Fifty-Three to Nineteen Hundred & One* (Dover, 1973).

Cohen, Barbara, et al, eds., *New York Observed: Artists & Writers Look at the City, 1650 to the Present* (Abrams, 1987).

Cudahy, Brian J., *Over and Back* (Fordham University Press, 1989).

Delaney, Edmund T., and Lockwood, Charles, *Greenwich Village: A Photographic Guide* (Dover, 1984).

Dolkart, Andrew S., *The Texture of TriBeCa* (TriBeCa Community Association, 1989).

Dunlap, David W., *On Broadway* (Rizzoli International, 1990).

Edmiston, Susan, and Cirino, Linda, *Literary New York* (Houghton Mifflin, 1976).

Fine, Jo R. and Wolfe, Gerard R., *The Synagogues of the Lower East Side* (New York University Press, 1978).

Furia, Philip, *The Poets of Tin Pan Alley* (Oxford University Press, 1990).

Gody, Lou, *The WPA Guide to New York City* (Pantheon, 1982).

Hood, Clifton, *722 Miles: The Building of the Subways and How They Transformed New York* (Simon & Schuster, 1993).

Kieran, John, *A Natural History of New York City* (Fordham, 1982).

Kinkead, Eugene, *Central Park: The Birth, Decline, and Renewal of a National Treasure* (Norton, 1990).

Leisner, Marcia, *Literary Neighborhoods of New York* (Starrhill Press, 1989).

Marquesee, Mike and Harris, Bill, eds., *New York: An Anthology* (Cadogan Publications, 1985).

Miller, Terry, *Greenwich Village and How It Got That Way* (Crown Publishers, 1990).

Moorhouse, Geoffrey, *Imperial City: New York* (H. Holt & Co., 1988).

Morris, Jan, *Manhattan '45* (Oxford University Press, 1987).

Plumb, Stephen, *The Streets Where They Lived* (MarLor Press, 1989).

Schermerhorn, Gene, *Letters to Phil* (New York Bound, 1982).

Shepard, Richard F., *Broadway from the Battery to the Bronx* (Harry N. Abrams, 1988).

Simon, Kate, *New York Places and Pleasures* (Meridien Books, 1959).

Snyder, Robert, *The Voice of the City: Vaudeville and Popular Culture in New York* (Oxford University Press, 1989).

Trager, James, *Park Avenue: Street of Dreams* (Atheneum Publishers, 1989).

Trager, James, *West of Fifth: The Rise and Fall of Manhattan's West Side* (Atheneum Publishers, 1987).

Economic, Political & Social History

Abbott, Berenice, *New York in the Thirties* (Dover, 1973).

Allen, Oliver E., *New York, New York: A History of the World's Most Exhilarating & Challenging City* (Macmillan, 1990).

Asbury, Herbert, *The Gangs of New York* (Capricorn Books, 1989).

Baldwin, James, *Notes of a Native Son* (Beacon Press, 1990).

Blackmar, Elizabeth, *Manhattan for Rent, Seventeen Eighty-five to Eighteen Fifty* (Cornell University Press, 1988).

Bender, Thomas, *New York Intellect: A History of Intellectual Life in New York City from 1750 to the Beginnings of Our Own Time* (University of Illinois Press, 1988).

Brandt, Nat, *The Man Who Tried to Burn New York* (Syracuse University Press, 1986).

Caro, Robert, *The Power Broker* (Vintage Books, 1975).

Cohen, B., Heller, S., and Chwast, S., *New York Observed* (Harry N. Abrams, 1987).

Douglas, Ann, *Terrible Honesty: Mongrel Manhattan in the 1920s* (Farrar, Straus, Giroux, 1995).

Ellis, Edward Robb, *The Epic of New York City: A Narrative History* (Old Town Books, 1966).

Feninger, Andreas, *New York in the Forties* (Dover, 1978).

Gambee, Robert, *Wall Street Christmas* (Norton, 1990).

Homberger, Eric, *The Historical Atlas of New York City* (Henry Holt, 1994).

Jacobs, William Jay, *Ellis Island* (Macmillan, 1990).

Kazin, Alfred, *Our New York* (Harper & Row Publishers, 1989).

Kessner, Thomas, *Fiorello H. La Guardia and the Making of Modern New York* (McGraw-Hill Publishing Co., 1989).

Kinkead, Gwen, *Chinatown: A Portrait of a Closed Society* (HarperCollins, 1992).

Koch, Edward, *Mayor: An Autobiography* (Simon & Schuster, 1984) and *Politics* (Simon & Schuster, 1986).

Kotker, Norman, *Ellis Island* (Macmillan, 1990).

Leeds, Mark, *Ethnic New York* (Passport Books, 1991).

Liebling, A. J., *The Telephone Booth Indian* (North Point Press, 1990).

MacKay, Ernst A., *The Civil War & New York City* (Syracuse University Press, 1990).

McCullough, David, *The Great Bridge* (Simon & Schuster, 1983).

Mitchell, Joseph, *Up in the Old Hotel* (Vintage, 1993).

Morris, Lloyd, *Incredible New York: High Life & Low Life of the Last Hundred Years* (Ayer Co. Publishers, 1975).

Patterson, Jerry E., *The Vanderbilts* (Harry N. Abrams, 1989).

Plunz, Richard A., *A History of Housing in New York City* (Columbia University Press, 1990).

Rink, Oliver A., *Holland on the Hudson* (New York State Historical Association, 1986).

Sanders, Ronald, *The Downtown Jews: Portraits of an Immigrant Generation* (Harper & Row, 1969).

Sante, Luc, *Low Life: Lures and Snares of Old New York* (Random House, 1991).

White, E. B., *Here Is New York* (Warner Books, 1988).

Architecture & The Arts

Alpern, Andrew, *Luxury Apartment Houses of Manhattan* (Dover, 1992).

Bogart, Michele H., *Public Sculpture and the Civic Ideal in New York City 1890–1989* (University of Chicago Press, 1989).

Boyer, M. Christine, *Manhattan Manners: Architecture & Style 1850–1900* (Rizzoli International, 1985).

Dolkart, Andrew S., *Guide to New York City Landmarks* (Preservation Press, 1992).

Gayle, Margot and Cohen, Michele, *Manhattan's Outdoor Sculpture* (Prentice Hall Press, 1988).

Gayle, Margot and Gillon, Edmund V., *Cast-Iron Architecture in New York* (Dover, 1974).

Goldberger, Paul, *The City Observed—New York: A Guide to the Architecture of Manhattan* (Vintage Books, 1979) and *Skyscraper* (Knopf, 1983).

Harrison, Marina and Rosenfeld, Lucy D., *Artwalks in New York* (Michael Kesend Publishing, 1991).

Lieberman, Nathaniel, *Manhattan Lightscape* (Abbeville Press, 1990).

Mackay, Donald A., *The Building of Manhattan: How Manhattan Was Built Overground & Underground, from the Dutch Settlers to the Skyscrapers* (Harper & Row Publishers, 1987).

Marshall, Richard, *Fifty New York Artists: A Critical Selection of Painters & Sculptors Working in New York* (Chronicle Books, 1986).

Orkin, Ruth, *More Pictures from My Window* (Rizzoli International, 1985).

Rajs, Jake, *Manhattan: An Island in Focus* (Rizzoli International, 1985).

Reed, Henry Hope and Sophia Duckworth, *Central Park: A History and a Guide* (Clarkson N. Potter, Inc., 1972).

Reynolds, Donald Martin, *The Architecture of New York* (Wiley, 1994).

Rosen, Laura, *Top of the City: New York's Hidden Rooftop World* (Thames & Hudson, 1990).

Salwen, Peter, *Upper West Side Story* (Abbeville Press, 1989).

Silver, Nathan, *Lost New York* (American Legacy, 1982).

Stern, Robert A. M., Gilmartin, Gregory, and Massengale, John M., *New York 1900: Metropolitan Architecture and Urbanism 1890–1915* (Rizzoli International, 1983).

Valenzi, Kathleen D., ed., *Private Moments: Images of Manhattan* (Howell Press, 1989).

von Pressentinwright, Carol, *Blue Guide New York* (W. W. Norton & Co., 1991).

Watson, Edward B., *New York Then & Now: Eighty-three Manhattan Sites Photographed in the Past & Present* (Dover Publications, 1976).

Willensky, Elliot, and White, Norval, *AIA Guide to New York City* (Harcourt Brace Jovanovich, 1989).

Fiction

Carr, Caleb, *The Alienist* (Random House, 1994).

Cooper, James F., *The Last of the Mohicans* (State University of New York Press, 1983).

Ellison, Ralph, *Invisible Man* (Random House, 1992).

Finney, Jack, *Time and Again* (Simon & Schuster, 1986) and *From Time to Time* (Simon & Schuster, 1995).

Fitzgerald, F. Scott, *The Great Gatsby* (Macmillan, 1981).

James, Henry, *New York Revisited* (Franklin Square Press, 1994) and *Washington Square* (G. K. Hall & Co., 1980).

Janowitz, Tama, *Slaves of New York* (Crown, 1986).

McInerney, Jay, *Bright Lights, Big City* (Random House, 1984).

Powell, Dawn, *The Locusts Have No King* (Yarrow Press, 1989).

Schine, Cathleen, *Rameau's Niece* (Plume, 1993).

Wharton, Edith, *The Age of Innocence* (Macmillan, 1994) and *Old New York* (Scribner, 1995).

Wolfe, Tom, *The Bonfire of the Vanities* (Farrar, Straus, Giroux, 1987).

Fiction for Kids

Barracca, Sal, *The Adventures of Taxi Dog* (Halcyon Books, 1990).

Gangloff, Deborah, *Albert and Victoria* (Crown Publishers, 1989).

Macaulay, David, *Underground* (Houghton Mifflin Co., 1976).

Selden, George, *The Cricket in Times Square* (Dell Publishing Co., 1970).

Swift, Hildegarde H., *The Little Red Lighthouse and the Great Gray Bridge* (Harcourt Brace Jovanovich, 1974).

Thomson, Kay, *Eloise* (Simon & Schuster, 1969).

Waber, Bernard, *Lyle, Lyle, Crocodile and the House on East 88th Street* (Houghton Mifflin Co., 1965).

White, E. B., *Stuart Little* (Harper & Row Publishers, 1973).

INDEX

Now Save Money On All Your Travels By Joining FROMMER'S™ TRAVEL BOOK CLUB
The World's Best Travel Guides
At Membership Prices!

Frommer's Travel Book Club is your ticket to successful travel! Open up a world of travel information and simplify your travel planning when you join ranks with thousands of value-conscious travelers who are members of the Frommer's *Travel Book Club*. Join today and you'll be entitled to all the privileges that come from belonging to the club that offers you travel guides for less to more than 100 destinations worldwide. **Annual membership is only $25.00 (U.S.) or $35.00 (Canada/Foreign).**

The Advantages of Membership:

1. Your choice of **three free** books (any **two** Frommer's Comprehensive Guides, Frommer's $-A-Day Guides, Frommer's Walking Tours or Frommer's Family Guides—plus **one** Frommer's City Guide, Frommer's City $-A-Day Guide or Frommer's Touring Guide).

2. Your own subscription to the **TRIPS & TRAVEL** quarterly newsletter.

3. You're entitled to a **30% discount** on your order of any additional books offered by the club.

4. You're offered (at a small additional fee) our **Domestic Trip-Routing Kits.**

Our **Trips & Travel** quarterly newsletter offers practical information on the best buys in travel, the "hottest" vacation spots, the latest travel trends, world-class events and much, much more.

Our **Domestic Trip-Routing Kits** are available for any North American destination. We'll send you a detailed map highlighting the best route to take to your destination—you can request direct or scenic routes.

Here's all you have to do to join:

Send in your membership fee of $25.00 ($35.00 Canada/Foreign) with your name and address on the form below along with your selections as part of your membership package to the address listed below. Remember to check off your three free books.

If you would like to order additional books, please select the books you would like and send a check for the total amount (please add sales tax in the states noted below), plus $2.00 per book for shipping and handling ($3.00 Canada/Foreign) to the address listed below.

FROMMER'S TRAVEL BOOK CLUB
P.O. Box 473
Mt. Morris, IL 61054-0473
(815) 734-1104

[ ] **YES!** I want to take advantage of this opportunity to join Frommer's Travel Book Club.

[ ] My check is enclosed. Dollar amount enclosed_____*
(all payments in U.S. funds only)

Name _____

Address _____

City _____ State _____ Zip _____

Phone ( )_____(In case we have a question regarding your order).

All orders must be prepaid.

To ensure that all orders are processed efficiently, please apply sales tax in the following areas: CA, CT, FL, IL, IN, NJ, NY, PA, TN, WA and CANADA.

*With membership, shipping & handling will be paid by Frommer's Travel Book Club for the three FREE books you select as part of your membership. Please add $2.00 per book for shipping & handling for any additional books purchased ($3.00 Canada/Foreign).

Allow 4-6 weeks for delivery for all items. Prices of books, membership fee, and publication dates are subject to change without notice. All orders are subject to acceptance and availability.

Please send me the books checked below:

FROMMER'S COMPREHENSIVE GUIDES

*(Guides listing facilities from budget to deluxe,
with emphasis on the medium-priced)*

	Retail Price	Code		Retail Price	Code
☐ Acapulco/Ixtapa/Taxco, 2nd Edition	$13.95	C157	☐ Jamaica/Barbados, 2nd Edition	$15.00	C149
☐ Alaska '94-'95	$17.00	C131	☐ Japan '94-'95	$19.00	C144
☐ Arizona '95 (Avail. 3/95)	$14.95	C166	☐ Maui, 1st Edition	$14.00	C153
☐ Australia '94'-'95	$18.00	C147	☐ Nepal, 2nd Edition	$18.00	C126
☐ Austria, 6th Edition	$16.95	C162	☐ New England '95	$16.95	C165
☐ Bahamas '94-'95	$17.00	C121	☐ New Mexico, 3rd Edition (Avail. 3/95)	$14.95	C167
☐ Belgium/Holland/ Luxembourg '93-'94	$18.00	C106	☐ New York State '94-'95	$19.00	C133
☐ Bermuda '94-'95	$15.00	C122	☐ Northwest, 5th Edition	$17.00	C140
☐ Brazil, 3rd Edition	$20.00	C111	☐ Portugal '94-'95	$17.00	C141
☐ California '95	$16.95	C164	☐ Puerto Rico '95-'96	$14.00	C151
☐ Canada '94-'95	$19.00	C145	☐ Puerto Vallarta/ Manzanillo/Guadalajara '94-'95	$14.00	C135
☐ Caribbean '95	$18.00	C148			
☐ Carolinas/Georgia, 2nd Edition	$17.00	C128	☐ Scandinavia, 16th Edition (Avail. 3/95)	$19.95	C169
☐ Colorado, 2nd Edition	$16.00	C143	☐ Scotland '94-'95	$17.00	C146
☐ Costa Rica '95	$13.95	C161	☐ South Pacific '94-'95	$20.00	C138
☐ Cruises '95-'96	$19.00	C150	☐ Spain, 16th Edition	$16.95	C163
☐ Delaware/Maryland '94-'95	$15.00	C136	☐ Switzerland/ Liechtenstein '94-'95	$19.00	C139
☐ England '95	$17.95	C159	☐ Thailand, 2nd Edition	$17.95	C154
☐ Florida '95	$18.00	C152	☐ U.S.A., 4th Edition	$18.95	C156
☐ France '94-'95	$20.00	C132	☐ Virgin Islands '94-'95	$13.00	C127
☐ Germany '95	$18.95	C158	☐ Virginia '94-'95	$14.00	C142
☐ Ireland, 1st Edition (Avail. 3/95)	$16.95	C168	☐ Yucatan, 2nd Edition	$13.95	C155
☐ Italy '95	$18.95	C160			

FROMMER'S $-A-DAY GUIDES

(Guides to low-cost tourist accommodations and facilities)

	Retail Price	Code		Retail Price	Code
☐ Australia on $45 '95-'96	$18.00	D122	☐ Israel on $45, 15th Edition	$16.95	D130
☐ Costa Rica/Guatemala/ Belize on $35, 3rd Edition	$15.95	D126	☐ Mexico on $45 '95	$16.95	D125
			☐ New York on $70 '94-'95	$16.00	D121
☐ Eastern Europe on $30, 5th Edition	$16.95	D129	☐ New Zealand on $45 '93-'94	$18.00	D103
☐ England on $60 '95	$17.95	D128	☐ South America on $40, 16th Edition	$18.95	D123
☐ Europe on $50 '95	$17.95	D127			
☐ Greece on $45 '93-'94	$19.00	D100	☐ Washington, D.C. on $50 '94-'95	$17.00	D120
☐ Hawaii on $75 '95	$16.95	D124			
☐ Ireland on $45 '94-'95	$17.00	D118			

FROMMER'S CITY $-A-DAY GUIDES

	Retail Price	Code		Retail Price	Code
☐ Berlin on $40 '94-'95	$12.00	D111	☐ Madrid on $50 '94-'95	$13.00	D119
☐ London on $45 '94-'95	$12.00	D114	☐ Paris on $50 '94-'95	$12.00	D117

FROMMER'S FAMILY GUIDES

(Guides listing information on kid-friendly hotels, restaurants, activities and attractions)

	Retail Price	Code		Retail Price	Code
☐ California with Kids	$18.00	F100	☐ San Francisco with Kids	$17.00	F104
☐ Los Angeles with Kids	$17.00	F103	☐ Washington, D.C. with Kids	$17.00	F102
☐ New York City with Kids	$18.00	F101			

FROMMER'S CITY GUIDES

(Pocket-size guides to sightseeing and tourist accommodations and facilities in all price ranges)

	Retail Price	Code		Retail Price	Code
☐ Amsterdam '93-'94	$13.00	S110	☐ Montreal/Quebec City '95	$11.95	S166
☐ Athens, 10th Edition (Avail. 3/95)	$12.95	S174	☐ Nashville/Memphis, 1st Edition	$13.00	S141
☐ Atlanta '95	$12.95	S161	☐ New Orleans '95	$12.95	S148
☐ Atlantic City/Cape May, 5th Edition	$13.00	S130	☐ New York '95	$12.95	S152
☐ Bangkok, 2nd Edition	$12.95	S147	☐ Orlando '95	$13.00	S145
☐ Barcelona '93-'94	$13.00	S115	☐ Paris '95	$12.95	S150
☐ Berlin, 3rd Edition	$12.95	S162	☐ Philadelphia, 8th Edition	$12.95	S167
☐ Boston '95	$12.95	S160	☐ Prague '94-'95	$13.00	S143
☐ Budapest, 1st Edition	$13.00	S139	☐ Rome, 10th Edition	$12.95	S168
☐ Chicago '95	$12.95	S169	☐ St. Louis/Kansas City, 2nd Edition	$13.00	S127
☐ Denver/Boulder/Colorado Springs, 3rd Edition	$12.95	S154	☐ San Diego '95	$12.95	S158
☐ Dublin, 2nd Edition	$12.95	S157	☐ San Francisco '95	$12.95	S155
☐ Hong Kong '94-'95	$13.00	S140	☐ Santa Fe/Taos/Albuquerque '95 (Avail. 2/95)	$12.95	S172
☐ Honolulu/Oahu '95	$12.95	S151	☐ Seattle/Portland '94-'95	$13.00	S137
☐ Las Vegas '95	$12.95	S163	☐ Sydney, 4th Edition	$12.95	S171
☐ London '95	$12.95	S156	☐ Tampa/St. Petersburg, 3rd Edition	$13.00	S146
☐ Los Angeles '95	$12.95	S164	☐ Tokyo '94-'95	$13.00	S144
☐ Madrid/Costa del Sol, 2nd Edition	$12.95	S165	☐ Toronto '95 (Avail. 3/95)	$12.95	S173
☐ Mexico City, 1st Edition	$12.95	S170	☐ Vancouver/Victoria '94-'95	$13.00	S142
☐ Miami '95	$12.95	S149	☐ Washington, D.C. '95	$12.95	S153
☐ Minneapolis/St. Paul, 4th Edition	$12.95	S159			

FROMMER'S WALKING TOURS

*(Companion guides that point out the places
and pleasures that make a city unique)*

	Retail Price	Code		Retail Price	Code
☐ Berlin	$12.00	W100	☐ New York	$12.00	W102
☐ Chicago	$12.00	W107	☐ Paris	$12.00	W103
☐ England's Favorite Cities	$12.00	W108	☐ San Francisco	$12.00	W104
☐ London	$12.00	W101	☐ Washington, D.C.	$12.00	W105
☐ Montreal/Quebec City	$12.00	W106			

SPECIAL EDITIONS

	Retail Price	Code		Retail Price	Code
☐ Bed & Breakfast Southwest	$16.00	P100	☐ National Park Guide, 29th Edition	$17.00	P106
☐ Bed & Breakfast Great American Cities	$16.00	P104	☐ Where to Stay U.S.A., 11th Edition	$15.00	P102
☐ Caribbean Hideaways	$16.00	P103			

FROMMER'S TOURING GUIDES

*(Color-illustrated guides that include walking tours,
cultural and historic sites, and practical information)*

	Retail Price	Code		Retail Price	Code
☐ Amsterdam	$11.00	T001	☐ New York	$11.00	T008
☐ Barcelona	$14.00	T015	☐ Rome	$11.00	T010
☐ Brazil	$11.00	T003	☐ Tokyo	$15.00	T016
☐ Hong Kong/Singapore/ Macau	$11.00	T006	☐ Turkey	$11.00	T013
☐ London	$13.00	T007	☐ Venice	$9.00	T014

---

*Please note: If the availability of a book is several months away, we may
have back issues of guides to that particular destination.
Call customer service at (815) 734-1104.*